# MENTAL TOUGHNESS FOR TEEN ATHLETES NUTRITION

A GUIDE TO HELPING TEENS IMPROVE
ATHLETIC PERFORMANCE, GAIN SELF-ESTEEM,
AND WELL-BEING THROUGH BETTER
NUTRITION

TOUGH TEEN ATHLETES
BOOK 2

LD HARRIS

# JOIN OUR COMMUNITY!

Join our exclusive Facebook Group and visit our website dedicated to empowering teen athletes with unparalleled mental toughness. Connect with a supportive community of athletes and parents, access expert advice, and gain insights that can give you a competitive edge. Don't miss out on this opportunity to transform your athletic journey—join us today! Scan the QR code!

# TOUGH TEEN ATHLETES CREDO

## TOUGH TEEN ATHLETES MISSION:

Our mission is to EMPOWER and EQUIP YOUNG ATHLETES with the mental resilience, physical training, and nutritional guidance necessary to excel in sports and life.

## TOUGH TEEN ATHLETES BELIEF:

We believe that **EACH ATHLETE** is **UNIQUE** and requires personalized training plans that address their specific physical and mental needs.

## TOUGH TEEN ATHLETES VISION:

We envision a world where **ALL** athletes receive **COMPREHENSIVE** support that addresses their **MENTAL, PHYSICAL,** and **EMOTIONAL** well-being, leading to success both on and off the field.

# DISCLAIMER

The publisher and author present this book "as is" and make no medical recommendations. We strongly advise consulting a healthcare professional before starting any exercise or nutrition program to ensure you are physically fit. The book provides educational insights into health, fitness, and nutrition and should not replace professional medical advice, diagnosis, or treatment. Always seek advice from a qualified healthcare provider for any concerns. Never disregard or delay seeking medical advice due to information in this book. Using the content is at your own risk, and we cannot guarantee it reflects the latest developments in the field.

# CONTENTS

*For my husband Kent, without your support none of my thoughts and dreams would ever come to fruition. Thank you.*

*For my kiddos, I couldn't be more proud of you both. You are the best kids any mom could ask for and have grown into amazing people.*

*Thanks all for humoring me when I ask, "where's your protein?" ;-)*

*LD & Mom*

# INTRODUCTION

If you looking to provide and your teen athlete with the best nutrition and make sure they have optimal mental health? Then you've come to the right place. In this book, LD Harris explains how eating good food is essential for a healthy mind and body in any athlete, especially teens. With the knowledge gained from this book, you'll be able to give your teen the best nutrition plan possible so they can fully thrive both physically and mentally in their sport and in life.

Armed with insight from our first book Mental Toughness for Teen Athletes, we now dig deeper into the critical topic of nutrition. We will show that these two issues, mental toughness and nutrition, are profoundly interconnected and should be addressed together. Through LD Harris' comprehensive guide, you'll be able to make the best nutrition choices for your teen to help them be successful in their athletic pursuits and lead a healthy lifestyle.

Parents and athletes should understand that nutrition and mental health are equally important for athletic performance.

Food impacts both the physical body and our mental well-being. This book explains how both, mental and physical health, can work together to reach peak performance and provides a comprehensive guide on properly nourishing your teenage athlete from both perspectives. Suppose you want to ensure that your teen athlete always has the energy and mental focus needed to excel in athletics and academics-In that case, it's time to focus on proper nutrition and the connection to mental well-being.

Just as a chef needs the right ingredients to prepare a delicious meal, teen athletes need the proper nutrition to reach their full potential. A balanced diet and adequate nutrition are essential for maintaining a healthy body and active mind. But it isn't just about eating healthy food to fuel the body; it also plays a critical role in mental health. By providing your child with proper nutrition, you empower them to take ownership of their physical and psychological well-being. In this book on nutrition for teen athletes, we explore how better dietary choices can help teen athletes feel energized and perform at their best – both on and off the field.

Teenage athletes have it tough. Not only do they have to work harder than their peers to stay at the top of their game, but they also face unique challenges in nutrition and meal management. Parents play a significant role in helping their teenage athletes stay healthy. They can provide guidance on proper nutrition, which is critical for any athlete as it helps them stay energized and focused during practices and games. Additionally, supplying the athlete's body with the proper nutrients for recovery is key to flourishing and growing while participating in sports. By working together, parents and teenage athletes can ensure that performance remains at its peak.

We assume you have a teen athlete in your house, work with teen athletes, or are a teen athlete yourself and don't want anything or anyone to hold them back from achieving their best and to gain that competitive edge. But one thing could be holding them back without you knowing: nutrition. The importance of proper nutrition for young athletes is often outside their training regime.

In this book, we focus on ensuring that teenage athletes get the optimal nutrition they need to perform at their highest level. This book covers topics such as: which foods fuel teen athletes and their ever-changing bodies, meal-prepping tips, and more for busy parents. If you want to ensure nothing comes between your teen athlete and their success, let me help you ensure they're eating right. With this book, you can give them the edge they deserve. I've often told athletes, "Although you may have the best training and exceptional skills, one of the key components to your success is your diet."

You'll find a comprehensive information on the nutritional needs of teenage athletes to ensure they get the nourishment they need to succeed in life. This book will help parents, coaches, and other mentors learn how to provide teens with the nutrition they need to fuel their growth and development. Topics like selecting nutrient-rich foods, managing portions for optimal performance, and understanding dietary restrictions have in-depth evaluation. By understanding these essential topics, adults can ensure that teenagers get the right balance of food to support their physical activities. Additionally, this book provides advice on cultivating a healthy relationship with food, from helping teens make informed decisions about what they eat to teaching them tools for emotional regulation.

We also cover why sleep is so vital for teenage athletes. Teens require more sleep than adults since they are still developing physically and mentally; getting enough sleep is essential for a teenager's physical and mental growth and development.

Read on to tackle the challenges of good nutrition and quality rest for all athletes!

# 1

## THE CONNECTION BETWEEN NUTRITION & MENTAL TOUGHNESS

The importance of nutrition in teenage athletes is like building a house. Food provides the essential materials and resources needed to construct a sturdy foundation for performance, both physically and mentally. Just like a home needs strong walls and supports to keep it standing, an athlete needs proper nutrition to thrive and stay healthy while training or competing. Furthermore, just as any form of damage or neglect can cause problems for a house, poor nutrition can lead to physical fatigue and mental health issues such as burnout, depression, stress, and anxiety in teen athletes. In this chapter, I will discuss how proper nutrition can create a positive environment for young athletes, leading to better overall performance.

TEEN ATHLETES OFTEN OVERLOOK the connection between mental toughness and nutrition. Nutrition plays a massive role in an athlete's overall performance, but many need to take the time to understand it. Contrary to popular belief, nutrition does play an essential role in mental toughness in sports. By fueling your teen athlete's body with the right foods, athletes can maintain focus, boost energy levels, provide their bodies with the nutrients needed to improve strength, endurance, and stay mentally tough to perform their best.

UNSURPRISINGLY, what you put in your body affects how you feel and perform. If your teen is trying to up their game in sports, it's essential to understand the impact of nutrition on their physical and mental performance. After all, athletes can only go as far as their physical strength and mental focus allow them; neglecting these vital components could mean they fall short of reaching their goals.

ENSURING your teen has a healthy diet rich in essential vitamins, minerals, fats, and carbohydrates is critical. If they're feeling sluggish or moody (have you ever met a hungry toddler?), it may be time for an overhaul. Eating nutrient-rich foods such as fruits, vegetables, lean proteins, and whole grains will give your teen the energy they need to compete and perform at their best. It's also essential that your teen stays well-hydrated, as dehydration can impact both physical performance and mental focus, leading to a drop in performance.

JUST LIKE WITH any other aspect of life, balance is vital when it comes to nutrition and sports performance. A diet that's too restrictive could lead to fatigue, resentment, and burnout over time, while a diet that's too indulgent can lead to poor energy levels, mental health issues, and slower reaction times.

LET'S face it - we all know that Mom and Dad are the ones that usually make sure everyone in the house is eating healthy. But when it comes to teenage athletes, sometimes parents need a helping hand. Since there's a link between mental cognition, mental toughness, and nutrition for teen athletes, you'll want to do your best as a parent to ensure they get enough nutritional value during their intensive training sessions. Eating the right food can help keep young minds sharp and focused during those intense workouts.

## UNDERSTANDING TEEN MENTAL DEVELOPMENT

MENTAL DEVELOPMENT IS an essential element in the growth and success of teen athletes. From understanding their skills and abilities to developing confidence and resilience, many different aspects come into play. Teens need a strong foundation in these areas to make the most of their athletic careers. Let us understand the various aspects of mental development in teen athletes and how they can help them achieve their goals.

## COGNITIVE DEVELOPMENT

COGNITIVE DEVELOPMENT IS a fascinating area of study. It's all about understanding how our brain works and how we learn, think, reason, and remember. We know that cognitive skills are vital in helping us navigate the world around us – it's how we solve problems, plan, and make decisions. That's why it's so important to understand how cognitive development works and what factors shape it throughout childhood and beyond.

(Lumen Learning, n.d.) We can break it down into three main
areas: intellectual functioning, language development, and
social cognition. Intellectual functioning is all about problem-
solving abilities like math or logic; language development
involves learning new words and improving communication
skills and conversational understanding, while social cognition
covers emotional intelligence, empathy, and self-awareness. All
these areas are interrelated, one helping shape the other as
teen athletes grow and develop. The teenage brain can be a
wild and unpredictable ride. With hormones raging, emotions
exploding, and the lure of independence beckoning, it's no
wonder teens go through some significant emotional growing
pains. But during adolescence, more is happening than just
mood swings; some genuine changes in cognitive development
are also taking place.

LET'S look at the basic facts about teen brain development. The
prefrontal cortex—the area responsible for decision-making
and impulse control—matures during this period. It's not
usually fully mature until the mid-20s. This stage in mental
development means that teens may not think before they act or
make rational decisions compared to adults. It also explains
why teenagers can often be impulsive or quick to anger - their
brains haven't yet developed enough to manage these feelings
appropriately.

As A PARENT, I've had the unfortunate experience of witnessing
my son's complete lack of rationality when traveling in a car
with friends. According to the Life360 app on his phone, the
vehicle traveled at an alarming speed - over 90mph! I was livid.
They were aware of the consequences their actions could have,
yet they still chose to ignore common sense and put themselves

(and others) in danger. Unfortunately, this is a reoccurring phenomenon among teenagers - rational behavior seems to take the back seat while impulsiveness takes charge.

MY EXPERIENCE with my son and his friends made me keenly aware of cognitive development in teenagers. The recklessness of their behavior, although they knew the consequences, was alarming. It made me realize that teens are still developing their problem-solving skills and rely heavily on external influences to help them make decisions. Their behavior prompted me to do more research into the cognitive development of teens and investigate how we, as parents, can support them in making responsible choices during this crucial period in their lives.

TEENAGERS TYPICALLY GO through common patterns and stages during their teenage years. In early adolescence, teens may become better at abstract thinking and problem-solving but struggle to understand complex social situations. Then in middle adolescence, teens begin to think more logically about their decisions and gain a better understanding of social relationships. Finally, late adolescence marks increased analytical skills and the ability to evaluate different perspectives—making it easier for teens to make balanced judgments and wise decisions. Additionally, this development also affects intellectual development. If you think your child is intelligent but struggling with abstract math problems, it's not that they're not smart enough, but their cognitive development isn't ready. Finally, no hard ages are associated with any of these development levels; each teenager is different, making parenting even more challenging.

IN ADDITION to these critical developmental milestones, parents of teen athletes should also focus on building positive habits that help promote healthy brain development in teen athletes. These healthy habits include getting enough sleep (essential for teenage brains), exercising regularly, and focusing on positive social relationships. These things can help foster a strong foundation for cognitive growth during the teen years and improve their mental health.

WHILE THE TEENAGE brain may not always make sense, it's important to remember that some genuine changes are taking place at this age—and understanding them can help us better support our teen athletes through this wild ride.

## PHYSICAL ACTIVITY & COMPETITIVE SPORTS

PHYSICAL ACTIVITY and competitive sports can be an excellent way for teens to stay mentally and physically healthy. Not only does exercise help them maintain their physical health, but it has also been linked to improved mental well-being. Studies have shown that those who engage in regular physical activity tend to have higher self-esteem, better social skills, and more positive body image than those who do not. Furthermore, studies have found that participating in competitive sports helps young people develop discipline, perseverance, and other essential life skills. These traits can help them succeed in school and provide a strong foundation for their future success. Additionally, engaging in physical activities may improve cognitive development, such as problem-solving skills. These factors combined make it clear that physical activity and competitive sports can be incredibly beneficial for teens' mental health and cognitive development.

SPECIFICALLY, a recent review highlighted that teens involved in team sports seemed to have better mental and social well-being than those who engaged in individual activities. They reported lower levels of anxiety, depression, and other social issues. So, more than the physical benefits of sports make them an excellent idea for teens. They can also provide some psychological perks. ("Teen Sports and Mental Health: 10 Mental Benefits of Sports," 2021)

## ACADEMIC PERFORMANCE

IT'S no secret that exercise is essential for physical health, but did you know it can also positively impact your teen athlete's academic performance? Studies show that students who stay active tend to do better in school by having higher grades, improved attendance records, enhanced cognitive abilities like memory, better behavior in the classroom, and staying focused better.

IT MAY SEEM PARADOXICAL, but children who juggle the time demands of athletics tend to become better at managing their hours. My kids are a testament to this: during the trying times of training and competing, they did better in school than when they weren't as busy. Limited time makes them focus on completing their academic tasks quickly and efficiently.

## BETTER COGNITIVE FUNCTION

A RECENT REVIEW determined that physical activity and fitness equals better cognitive function in children. They're also faster and more accurate thinkers than their peers. Even better, a good workout can help them ace tests in school. If you want your teen athlete to become an academic superstar, getting moving is the way to go.

STUDIES HAVE CONSISTENTLY SHOWN that regular physical exercise positively affects brain plasticity, which can help improve cognitive abilities and mental well-being. In other words: your teen will be brighter, healthier, and happier as they stay active. Get them out there hitting those balls and running those laps today - because studies show 'Physical Exercise' pays off in the long run. Or try an activity they've never done before to keep them active and expose them to a new way of moving their body and cross-training for their sport.

## THE ROLE NUTRITION & MENTAL TOUGHNESS

MENTAL TOUGHNESS: it's a phrase that gets bandied around quite a lot in sports circles, but what does it mean? Mental toughness is staying focused and motivated despite challenges or setbacks. It's about pushing yourself when your energy is running low, being resilient in the face of adversity, and never giving up.

MENTAL TOUGHNESS ISN'T something a teen athlete is born with, but it is something they can learn. The 4 C's of mental toughness are vital components to develop the hardiness that will keep them focused and moving forward through any obstacles life throws their way.

- *Control* means having the power to manage thoughts, feelings, and behaviors to reach desired goals. Building up control takes practice and determination; practice focusing on what's within your power instead of dwelling on external factors.
- *Commitment* is essential if you want to be mentally tough. When one Commits, it means devotion to a particular goal or mission without wavering despite adversity or opposition. It requires focus and dedication to an end goal, even when faced with difficulty.
- *Confidence* is fundamental to success in any field, including sports. Self-belief and trust in one's ability are the foundations of confidence. Knowing you can handle anything your way is a powerful mental toughness tool.
- *Challenge* yourself regularly by pushing boundaries and striving for more than what you think is possible. Impossible achieves nothing, so embrace challenges as an opportunity to work towards something greater than where you currently stand.

MENTAL TOUGHNESS ISN'T something teens magically acquire overnight - it requires dedication and practice, just like any other skill! But with these 4 C's in mind, they'll be well on their way to achieving success, whatever life throws at them.

FOR PARENTS OF TEEN ATHLETES, mental toughness in sports is not a one-size-fits-all concept. It's important to remember that showing weakness or vulnerability doesn't mean someone isn't mentally tough – quite the opposite. Vulnerability and openness are qualities associated with strong mental toughness because it takes courage to open up and confront fears. So don't think your kid needs to have an unshakable invincible mindset from day one -instead, encourage them to embrace the journey of becoming mentally tougher every single day. (Mental Toughness: The Key to Athletic Success, n.d.)

## MENTAL HEALTH VS MENTAL TOUGHNESS

PARENTS OF TEEN athletes have likely heard the terms "mental health" and "mental toughness" thrown around. Is there a difference between these two concepts?

MENTAL HEALTH IS all about taking care of your mental well-being, such as getting enough sleep, eating healthy food, and having a balanced lifestyle. Mental toughness is leveraging psychology to push yourself through challenging tasks and situations with resilience, courage, and optimism. It's not necessarily about suppressing negative thoughts or feelings—it's about learning how to stay focused and motivated when things are intimidating or challenging.

TEACHING your child how to cultivate both aspects of their mental game can help them become an even better athlete. By understanding the importance of mental health and mental toughness, your teen can develop the skill set to carry them through those grueling practices and demanding games.

## LINK BETWEEN NUTRITION & MENTAL HEALTH

PARENTS OF ATHLETES should be aware of the connection between nutrition, mental health, and mental toughness. Eating a balanced diet helps optimize physical performance and supports cognitive functions that can empower athletes with greater mental resilience.

REGARDING TEENS, proper nutrition is even more critical as they develop brains and bodies. Ensure your teen athletes get nutrients through a balanced diet to support physical and psychological development! A balanced diet will help build their physical strength and mental toughness - an essential trait for any athlete looking to excel in their sport. (Eating to Boost Energy, 2011) Poor nutrition can lead to various cognitive issues, including mental health. Decreased ability to make decisions, slow down reaction times, fatigue, increased stress, and increased anxiety.

## ENERGY LEVELS & CONCENTRATION

GOOD NUTRITION IS vital for teen athletes' mental toughness and overall success. Eating the right foods helps keep energy levels high and keeps concentration sharp. When teens fuel their bodies with nutrient-rich food, they can make split-second decisions on the court or field. Eating healthy also ensures that teens don't run out of breath quickly when competing, which could put them at a disadvantage. Parents should ensure that their teen athletes eat well-rounded meals and snacks throughout the day — this will give them an edge when pushing through tough, athletic competition.

## STRESS MANAGEMENT

IT'S no secret that the link between nutrition and mental toughness for teen athletes is strong. Eating a balanced diet can make a huge difference in their daily energy levels and ability to manage stress. Parents of teen athletes should ensure they understand the importance of proper nutrition and know how it contributes to their performance both on and off the field. As most coaches will tell you, what your kids fuel themselves with before and after a game impacts their performance - so be sure to have them eating right. And if all else fails, remind them about the famous quote from Michael Jordan: "The talent you have is God-given, but the skill is developed by hours and hours of practice." That includes fueling up with healthy eats. It's time for parents to help their teen athletes get the proper nutrition to reach peak performance.

## SLEEP QUALITY AND RECOVERY

SLEEP IS an essential part of life and significantly affects how well athletes perform. When teens don't get enough sleep, their bodies can't adequately recover from previous workouts and start feeling sluggish. When we sleep is when we get stronger. That's why nutrition, rest, and mental toughness are connected

— if your teen isn't getting the proper nutrients or enough rest, it could affect their performance on the field or court. Ensure your teen is eating nutritious meals full of vitamins and minerals to help them stay energized throughout the day and aim for eight hours PLUS of quality sleep each night so they're ready to tackle any challenge. Poor nutrition can adversely affect their sleep, creating a vicious cycle between poor eating habits, poor sleep quality, and poor mental health.

THIS CHAPTER EXPLAINS the integral part proper nutrition plays in not only physical health, but, also, our mental health. Furthermore, understanding the importance of rest and recovery is invaluable for proper physical and mental development. Now that you're familiar with these connections let's explore some common myths surrounding food, fuel, and performance for athletes.

# 2

## DEBUNKING NUTRITION MYTHS

Teen athletes have unique nutrition needs, but unfortunately, there are too many myths about what they should be eating. Parents can feel overwhelmed and confused trying to understand the most appropriate diet for their athlete's performance and health. Don't worry – I'm here to help bust these nutrition myths and provide you with the facts. (Nutrition for Teens, 2022) From understanding protein requirements to debunking calorie counting myths, I'll arm you with knowledge so that you can help your teen athlete stay strong, healthy, and perform at their best. Let's get started on shattering those nutritional misconceptions.

### MYTH:
### Game Performance Isn't Affected by What Your Teen Athlete Eats

### FACT:
*Eating the Right Foods Before and After Activity Can Help Athletes Perform Better*

FOODS LIKE OATS, fruits, and vegetables provide energy, while lean proteins like fish, chicken breasts, and egg whites will help with muscle repair. Studies have shown that athletes who get adequate nutrition perform better than those who don't. Eating healthy meals and snacks before and after a practice or game can give you more energy and help you play at your best.

ADDING healthy foods to your daily diet ensures your body has all the nutrients needed to perform best during practices and games. Whenever I'd attend a swim meet, baseball tournament, or an all-day competition, I would be dismayed to see the snack table stocked with candy bars, fruit snacks, and Gatorade - not ideal fuel for athletes of any age. It was particularly upsetting to observe young athletes guzzling high-sugar sports drinks and munching on Nerd Ropes between races; this hurt their performance and hindered their mental capabilities amid the stress-inducing competition. Despite my strong disapproval of such unhealthy snacking habits, I still occasionally succumbed to temptation and purchased sugary treats for my kids. However, I have always made sure that they had a healthy snack before, and they ate their sugary treat AFTER the meet. Also, I reminded them that what they put in their bodies is crucial to their success. I urge all parents, guardians, and athletes to maintain a healthy diet for peak performance actively.

### MYTH:
**It Doesn't Matter What Players Eat After Games**

### FACT:
*Eating an Appropriate Meal Within 30 minutes of Exercise is Vital to Better Health, Recovery, and Performance*

16

CHOOSE nutrient-rich snacks such as yogurt, fruit smoothies with protein powder, or homemade protein bars for your teen athletes. Eating the right foods after an intense workout or sporting event is essential to ensure that muscles recover properly and are ready for future activity. It's necessary to ensure that your teen athlete's post-game meals balance carbohydrates and protein to replenish energy stores and muscle repair. That means digging into lean proteins like chicken, fish, Greek yogurt, tofu, eggs, or beans paired with complex carbohydrates such as whole wheat pasta, quinoa, brown rice, or sweet potatoes.

## MYTH:
### Athletes Get Enough Protein from What They Eat

## FACT:
### *Athletes Need Help to get the Daily Recommended Amount of Protein*

THE COMMON MISCONCEPTION regarding teenage athletes and nutrition is that they get enough protein from their diets. This isn't true , especially if they're on a calorie-restricted diet for weight loss.– unless you are filling your teen athlete's plate with steaks, eggs, fish, or beans for breakfast, lunch, and dinner. Getting enough protein was a massive challenge for us with our son. He is naturally very lean; during swim season, he had protein at every meal and snack, and still, his body fat fell from 6%, which is low already, to 3%. He confessed that sometimes "he just doesn't have the energy to eat." If you think low blood sugar was a cause of his fatigue, you'd be correct. It was a vicious cycle. Teenage athletes need to get more protein than the average person because of the extra physical exertion they put themselves through. Studies have shown that adolescent athletes should consume around 1 gram of protein per pound of body weight daily to maintain muscle mass and repair muscle damage, which is normal, caused by intense training. Don't worry about them having to eat steak 24/7 – they can get plenty of proteins from various sources such as nuts, legumes, yogurt, milk, and tofu.

ANOTHER COMMON MISCONCEPTION is that teenage athletes must take protein supplements to succeed in their sport. While some supplements can help, teen athletes should use them with caution and under the guidance of a doctor or sports performance nutritionist. A balanced diet that provides enough vitamins, minerals, proteins, and carbohydrates is usually enough to fuel an athlete's performance without additional supplements.

## MYTH:
### Coaches Shouldn't Worry about What Players Eat

## FACT:
*Coaches should teach proper nutrition so that teenage athletes make good food choices at home and when eating out with friends.*

IT'S a common misconception that coaches don't have to worry about adolescent athletes' nutrition. Sure, it's not the coach's job to feed the players and ensure they're eating healthy daily, but sports nutrition is essential to any teenage athlete's performance. Eating right helps manage energy levels during practice and competition but also helps build muscle mass, improve speed and agility, and reduce the risk of injury. Poor nutrition can lead to fatigue during longer practices or games, decreased energy levels, and slower reaction and recovery times from physical activity.

COACHES, you can and should encourage your athletes to make wise nutritional choices before, during, and after workouts. Teach them how certain foods can help them perform better and provide healthy snacks for them to have on hand. Teaching teens how to read a nutrition label is also vital in assisting them to understand the nutritional content of certain foods. They should also be hydrated throughout the day – not just during practice or games. Talk to your players about how nutrition isn't only important during physical activity but that it helps with overall health and well-being. I frequently give talks on sports performance and nutrition to teen athlete teams, which help teen athletes see the connection between what they eat and how well they perform and help them make positive choices. See if one is available in your area to give a talk.

BY EDUCATING players about sports nutrition, coaches are helping teen athletes make the most of their training and reach peak performance. If teenage athletes have the right fuel, they'll be well-prepared for any challenge.

### MYTH:
**The Body is the Best Indicator of When to Drink Water**

### FACT:
*Waiting until Feeling Thirsty means Mild Dehydration has Already Started*

TEENAGE ATHLETES MUST STAY HYDRATED; the recommended amount of water is 8-10 glasses daily. But there's no "magic number" for how much water teenagers should drink. Your body is not the best indicator of when you need to rehydrate. Of course, if you start feeling thirsty, it's time for a glass. One of the best indicators of dehydration is urine output and color. If your teen athlete has dark urine and low production, they most likely are dehydrated.

PARENTS OF TEEN athletes need to know that every teenager's needs are different. What works for one person may not work as well for someone else. That means it's up to individual teens (and their parents) to pay attention and tailor their water intake to their active lifestyle. Some foods can replenish fluids as well. Soups, some fruits, and some vegetables can also provide fluids. Additionally, electrolytes and hydration drinks, just watching the sugar and chemical content, can be an excellent choice for particularly active teens who need an extra energy boost during practice.

### MYTH:
### Carbohydrates Cause Weight Gain

### FACT:
*Carbohydrates are an essential energy source for athletes, providing them the fuel they need to perform at their best.*

ONE OF THE most common misconceptions among parents of teenage athletes is that carbohydrates cause weight gain. This thought couldn't be further from the truth. Eating healthy carbs like oatmeal, quinoa, and sweet potatoes can help teen athletes stay energized throughout their workouts and games.

Furthermore, when paired with proteins like chicken breast, grass-fed beef, or fish, these carbohydrates provide essential nutrients that build muscle mass and optimize performance. Please don't worry about carbs making your athlete gain weight - eating a balanced diet full of healthy carbs will only benefit them in the long run, improving their performance and mental health.

## MYTH:
### Eating a Low-Fat Diet is Healthy for Weight Management

## FACT:
### Fats are Essential to Providing Energy for Activity

FATS ARE essential to provide energy and help the absorption of fat-soluble vitamins like A, D, E, and K. Healthy fats such as olive oil, nuts, and fatty fish, like salmon, should be included in your teenager's diet. Avoid trans fats from processed food items like chips and pastries.

PARENTS OF TEEN athletes may be under the impression that a low-fat diet is the best way to manage their child's weight and health. But this thought process needs to be corrected. A diet that is too low in fat can lead to a lack of energy, hormone imbalances, and decreased performance on the field. To ensure healthy nutrition for teenage athletes, focus on a balanced diet with a good mix of all macronutrients – healthy fats included. Sources of healthy fats include nuts, seeds, avocados, olive oil, and fish. Focusing on nutrient-dense whole foods such as fruits, vegetables, and lean proteins will also provide essential vitamins and minerals for optimal performance. Regarding weight management, it is important to encourage teens to stay active and engage in healthy habits – not just restrict their diet. Strive for a balance of nutrition and physical activity for optimal health!

BY FOCUSING on a balanced diet with plenty of whole foods, teenage athletes can reach the peak of their performance without compromising their health. With this approach, there will be no need for any false "low-fat" myths.

## MYTH:
### All Supplements are Safe

## FACT:
### *Supplements may Contain Hidden Ingredients or Even Dangerous Chemicals.*

One of the most pervasive myths about sports nutrition for teen athletes is that all supplements are safe. Unfortunately, this isn't necessarily true; the FDA does not regulate many supplements. Those supplements may contain hidden ingredients or even dangerous chemicals. Parents should know what their teenagers are taking and research any supplement they consider adding to their diets. A sports performance nutritionist can fill in the gaps and provide an informed opinion on which supplements are beneficial.

WHILE IT'S essential to understand the risks associated with certain supplements, it's also crucial to remember that a balanced diet is still the best source of nutrition for teen athletes. While additional supplementation may be necessary depending on a particular athlete's needs, there's no substitute for the right combination of fruits, vegetables, whole grains, proteins, and healthy fats. A sports performance nutritionist can help create a plan meeting an athlete's needs.

## MYTH:
## Teen Athletes Must Work Out Every Day and Eat "Clean" to be Healthy

### FACT:
*Eating Non-Clean Foods Occasionally is OK AND taking a REST Day is Necessary*

IT'S a common misconception that teenage athletes must work out daily and eat "clean" to be healthy. But the truth is, there's no one-size-fits-all approach to nutrition for teenagers. Some days it's excellent – even beneficial – to take a rest day from physical activity or indulge in an occasional treat.

FOR PARENTS OF TEEN ATHLETES, it's important to remember that exercise should serve as a means for self-expression and enjoyment, not just a guilt trip. Eating "clean" all the time doesn't always lead to healthier habits – if anything, it can create an unhealthy obsession with food and body image. Instead of strict diets, encourage your teen to focus on a balanced diet that includes all the essential food groups. Ensure their meals include fruits, vegetables, proteins, and healthy carbs like whole grains. Various foods will provide them with energy for physical activity and help them meet their daily nutritional needs.

REMIND your teen that it's okay to indulge in an occasional treat or two – within reason. Eating treats shouldn't be considered "bad" behavior but should be part of a balanced lifestyle.

## MYTH:
### Endurance Athletes don't Need as Much Protein as Strength-Trained Athletes

## FACT:
### *Endurance Athletes DO need Protein*

It's a common misconception that endurance athletes don't need as much protein in their diet as strength-trained athletes. This idea is not accurate. Protein is an essential nutrient for all athletes, regardless of the type of competition. Protein helps build muscle and aids in recovery after exercise. Teenage athletes should get 10-35% of their daily calories from lean proteins such as fish, poultry, tofu, legumes, and nuts. Ensure those endurance teen athletes get enough protein in their diets-it'll help them reach their performance goals!

## MYTH:
### Teen Athletes Shouldn't Eat After Dinner

## FACT:
### *Teen Athletes NEED Calories*

SOME PARENTS of teenage athletes might think their kids shouldn't eat after dinner, but they must ensure their athletes eat enough throughout the day. Eating a light snack in the evening can help replenish energy stores for the next day's activities and support muscle growth. Healthy snacks like yogurt and fresh fruit will provide the perfect balance of protein, carbs, and healthy fats to keep them fueled. Eating a healthy snack before bed may help your teen athlete get the restorative sleep they need.

PARENTS MAY WANT teen athletes to avoid junk food altogether, but this isn't always realistic - or necessary! Allowing teenagers an occasional treat can be beneficial for them. Moderation is vital - eating the occasional slice of cake or pizza doesn't ruin their diet. If they're eating a balanced diet and getting enough exercise, these foods are okay in moderation. For example, cereal never was eaten at our house for breakfast; it's too full of sugar to have in the morning, so at our house, cereal was eaten, with organic whole milk, for dessert.

ANOTHER MISCONCEPTION IS that teenage athletes must obsessively count calories or measure portions. While it may be helpful for teens to track what they eat regarding performance and emotions, counting every calorie can lead to unhealthy habits. Instead, encourage teen athletes to get enough variety - lean proteins, healthy fats, complex carbs, and plenty of fruits and vegetables - without worrying about exact portion sizes.

## MYTH:
### Sports Drinks Provide Superb Rehydration

## FACT:
*Sports Drinks are LOADED with Undesirable Ingredients*

ONE OF THE biggest misconceptions about nutrition for teenage athletes is that sports drinks benefit their health. On the one hand, these drinks may provide an athlete with a quick burst of energy and hydration, but on the other hand, they contain high levels of sugar, which can lead to weight gain, promote tooth decay, and mess with blood sugar levels. Parents must understand that their teen athletes don't need to rely on sports drinks to stay active during exercise or replenish lost electrolytes after activity.

FRUITS, vegetables, and whole grains are some of the best sources of carbohydrates that help keep your teen athlete energized throughout the day. Foods such as oatmeal, sweet potatoes, apples, oranges, and bananas all contain natural sugars that are healthier than sugar in sports drinks. Additionally, proteins can help your teen athletes build muscle and recover quickly after physical activity.

## MYTH:
### You Should Consume Sugary Foods During a Game for Energy

### FACT:
*Sugary Foods will Spike Blood Sugar and Create a CRASH*

WHILE THESE FOODS can provide a sudden burst of energy, they won't give you any long-term benefits—in fact, they could do more harm than good. Healthy foods like fruits, vegetables, lean proteins, and whole grains will provide lasting energy throughout your day and help fuel your performance.

## MYTH:
### Being Overweight will make You Too Heavy for Sports

## FACT:
### *Being Overweight Doesn't Mean You Can't Be a GREAT Athlete*

BEING overweight doesn't necessarily mean you can't be a great athlete—it just means you must pay closer attention to what foods you eat and how often. Eating a balanced diet with plenty of whole grains, fruits, vegetables, lean proteins, and healthy fats is essential for any athlete looking to improve their performance.

# 3

## FUELING WITH INTENT

Nutrition is the cornerstone of a healthy life; it is essential to understand what you're putting into your body each day. While some foods are healthy and provide crucial nutrients, others are best in moderation. Eating a balanced diet with the right mix of proteins, carbohydrates, fats, vitamins, minerals, and water can help keep your teen athlete in good physical shape and give their brain the fuel it needs to stay sharp and develop properly.

IT DOESN'T HAVE to be complicated or tedious - plenty of delicious recipes will help you get all the nutrition you need! Add more vegetables to their plate, packed with vitamins, minerals, and fiber. Fruits are also excellent sources of natural sugars and antioxidants; just be sure to eat them in moderation. Protein in meat, dairy, and eggs is a crucial component of a healthy diet; it's vital for muscle tissue and cell growth. Whole grains are also packed with essential vitamins, minerals, and fiber - try switching out refined white bread or pasta for healthier whole- wheat options.

REMEMBER fats - they're an essential part of your diet also. Healthy fats can help support brain health and provide energy throughout the day; add nuts, seeds, or avocados to your meals. Be mindful of saturated fat intake as well – these fats are typically in fast foods. Drinking plenty of water is essential for staying hydrated and keeping your organs functioning properly.

## IMPORTANCE OF NUTRITION in Teen Athletes

FOR TEEN ATHLETES to be at their peak performance and get the most from their athletic pursuits, they must fuel up on the right foods. That means not just grabbing a snack before practice - but making sure it will give them the energy they need for success. With some creativity, you can ensure your teen athlete gets all the nutrition they need without sacrificing taste or variety.

## LUNCHTIME AT SCHOOL

AS A FORMER HIGH SCHOOL TEACHER, I had ample opportunity to observe the lunchtime offerings. What I encountered shocked me - greasy cheese pizza paired with marinara dipping sauce serving as the vegetable? YUCK! And yes, you read that correctly. All those carbohydrates paired with a small amount of protein would send their blood sugar through the roof! It was no wonder many of them were flagging in my afternoon classes and during afternoon practices. As such, my children took sack lunches to school every day they attended. While my son may have initially considered this uncool (what adolescent doesn't?), he eventually saw its many benefits - financial savings chief among them. But beyond that, it allowed him more control over his diet and encouraged experimentation in the kitchen. In short, it provided an invaluable learning experience. For my part, I could rest assured that his lunch packed nutritious foods - and that's priceless.

LUNCHTIME IN SCHOOL is a time for energizing and refueling the body. However, this is often not the case when it comes to the lunches served in schools today, especially for teen athletes. The lunches offered provide little nutritional value, with processed foods high in sugar and trans-fats making up much of what's available. These lunches deprive many young people of essential nutrients to help them reach their peak physical performance and support their emotional and mental growth and health. With so much at stake, it's no wonder that nutrition-minded parents are concerned about their children's diets while at school. But even those who understand the importance of eating healthy may feel overwhelmed by the challenge of finding nutritious alternatives. There are a few options, however—such as bringing packed lunches from home, seeking healthier school lunch options, or advocating for nutritional reform in the cafeteria.

NUTRITION IS JUST as crucial for teen athletes as it is for other age groups, if not more so. It plays a vital role in helping teens perform better, stay healthy, and prevent injuries. Eating the right foods can help athletes recover faster from physical activity, improve their mental focus, mental health, and increase endurance levels. In addition to fueling muscle growth and repair, eating balanced meals will promote overall health.

A Nutritious Diet Should Include:

- *Lean proteins* like grass-fed beef, chicken, turkey, fish, or eggs.
- *Complex carbohydrates* such as quinoa, brown rice, or oatmeal.
- *Vegetables* of all kinds.
- *Dairy products* like milk or yogurt.
- *Good fats* like avocado and olive oil.

Some nutritionists/dietitians believe that low-fat dairy is the way to go. I disagree- the nutrients in dairy are "attached" to the fat in dairy. Drinking whole milk provides nutrients that all bodies need. The fat helps slow digestion and keep blood sugar levels from spiking. If you want to get those essential nutrients for your teen athletes, don't cut the fat-whole milk, in my opinion, is the way to go. Low-fat dairy can be an excellent option for some people, but it shouldn't be considered the only choice. Whole milk has been around forever and still provides vital vitamins and minerals our bodies need. Teen athletes should also get plenty of fruits and vegetables daily to give the body essential vitamins and minerals.

It is also essential for teen athletes to stay hydrated when engaging in physical activity, as dehydration can affect performance levels. Drinking plenty of water throughout the day will help keep teens energized and alert while avoiding sugary beverages and energy drinks that contain high amounts of caffeine and sugar.

REGARDING TEENAGE ATHLETES, nutrition is not just important – it's essential. Eating the right foods helps young athletes fuel their bodies with the energy and nutrients they need to perform at their best. It also helps keep them healthy to stay in the game longer! Good nutrition isn't complicated or expensive; all it takes is a bit of planning and dedication.

## NUTRITION ANALYSIS

NUTRITION ISN'T JUST about counting calories; it's also a lot to do with the micronutrients and macronutrients that make up food. Micronutrients are vitamins, minerals, and trace elements, while macronutrients include carbohydrates, proteins, and fats. It's essential to pay attention to all these elements when eating healthily. Planning meals to provide the nourishment your teen athletes, you, and your bodies need. The trick is finding a balance between them all.

# 4

## MACRONUTRIENTS

Carbohydrates are one of the three main macronutrients that make up our food. They are sugar and come in complex carbs (like grains, legumes, and starchy vegetables) and simple carbs (like fruit and honey). Complex carbs provide slow-release energy for steady fuel throughout the day, while simple carbs can give us an instant energy kick. Eating a variety of carbohydrates is the best bet for sustained energy. For example: Eat some yummy whole grain toast (complex carbohydrate) with some nut butter (protein) and add a dollop of honey (simple carbohydrate) for sweetness, and you've got a well-rounded meal/snack. Ensure you include plenty of fruits and veggies; pack with good nutrients and fiber to keep you full longer.

IF YOU'RE LOOKING to properly fuel your athlete, you should understand that carbohydrates are essential to your child's diet for a few different reasons:

- ___Carbs provide energy___ to help them power through their sports practice and games.
- ___Carbs can help replenish the glycogen stores___ in muscle cells after exercise, which helps with recovery.
- ___Carbs also help maintain optimal performance___ by providing fuel and helping your body regulate its temperature so it doesn't overheat during workouts or competitions.
- ___They stabilize blood sugar___ to prevent cravings and fatigue during the day.

SINCE ALL CARBS aren't created equal, ensure your teen athlete gets enough complex carbohydrates from whole grains, fruits, vegetables, and legumes to support their active lifestyle. When it comes to how much carbohydrates young athletes should be eating, this varies based on the individual's age, weight, gender, and physical activity level.

USE THESE GUIDELINES FOR CARBOHYDRATE CONSUMPTION:

- ___45-65% of daily calories from carbohydrates___.
- ___Pre-Training or Competition-Time___ carb consumption-1-4 hours before exercise or competition as this will help restore muscle glycogen levels.
- ___During training or competition___, athletes can benefit from consuming 30-60 grams of carbs per hour to maintain blood glucose levels and help delay fatigue. Keeping blood sugar levels stable is so important in tournaments, swims, and track meets,

where competition occurs after a break that can be as long as a few hours.

- **_Post-training or competition_** athletes should aim to consume 1.2-1.5 grams of carbohydrates per kilogram of body weight within 30 minutes after a workout or competition; this helps start the muscle recovery process, and restore glycogen stores lost during the activity.

## FATS

FATS ARE essential for teenage athletes. Eating fat is not only okay, but it's also beneficial for everybody. Fats provide teen athletes with sustained energy since they are slow to digest and are caloric-dense, meaning they offer many calories per gram. Additionally, fats are essential for proper growth and development and for maintaining healthy cells, organs, and skin. Fats also help absorb specific vitamins and minerals that boost immunity. They also make food taste better so your teen athlete can get more enjoyment out of their meals. Plus, research has shown that healthy fats can help lower cholesterol levels and reduce the risk of certain diseases.

## HEALTHY FATS

SOME OF THE best fats for teen athletes include nuts, seeds, avocados, olive oil, and salmon. Nuts are full of healthy monounsaturated fat, which helps to keep muscles functioning well. Seeds provide essential fatty acids and vitamins that aid concentration. Avocado is packed full of B vitamins which help to convert food into energy. Olive oil provides an energy boost, and salmon is an excellent source of omega-3 fatty acids, which help reduce inflammation.

## Unhealthy Fats

Fried foods, processed meats, and margarine are all high in saturated and trans fats, which can increase bad cholesterol levels and inflammation. To ensure your child gets the best nutrition possible for their sports activities, limit their intake of these types of food. (Infront, 2019) While some fats are great for giving teenage athletes the energy boost they need, others might leave them sluggish. (Wynn, 2020) However, saturated fats are not all bad, as full-fat organic dairy, grass-fed beef, and coconut are full of healthy nutrients for a growing body.

Choosing the suitable types of fats for your teenage athlete is critical to getting the most out of their training sessions. Additionally, the information gathered in your teen athlete's food, sleep, training, and performance log will help you determine which foods work well for them.

## Protein

Protein is an essential part of a well-rounded diet for teens who are active in sports. Not only does protein provide energy and strength to build muscles, but it also helps repair tissues after strenuous physical activity.

NO MATTER how old your athlete is, protein is essential to any athlete's diet. But when it comes to teenage athletes in particular, protein becomes even more critical. Not only do they have the physical demands of training and competition, but their bodies and brains are quickly growing. Eating the right amount and type of protein can help your teen train more efficiently and stay healthy. Teens should strive to have a balanced meal containing protein at each mealtime. Before or after exercise is also a great time to get some extra protein into the mix, think smoothies with Greek yogurt or hummus on crackers.

THE BEST PROTEIN sources for teen athletes come from fish and grass-fed meats, dairy products such as yogurt and cheese, and eggs. Plant-based proteins like beans, tofu, nuts and nut butter, seeds, and quinoa also provide excellent energy sources. Additionally, plant-based proteins pack fiber and minerals to support your teen's overall health and performance. Ensuring your teen athlete eats various proteins daily will ensure they stay fueled during practice or competition. (Protein for the Teen Athlete, n.d.)

WITH SO MANY fantastic options out there for teenage athletes to try out, finding delicious ways to get in those essential nutrients has never been easier.

NUT BUTTERS ARE one of my favorite proteins to incorporate into my daily nutrition regime. Nut butter provides an excellent source of protein. Nut butter can integrate easily into anyone's daily diet with whole-grain sandwiches, apples and nut butter, smoothies, and more, making them a perfect meal or snack for busy athletes. Also, nut butter contains various essential vitamins and minerals that help strengthen the immune system while aiding muscle growth and development. Various nut butters are currently available in most grocery stores, including peanut, almond, cashew, sunflower (a seed), and other options. The key is finding the one that best suits your athlete's needs and likes.

## Too Much Protein

Too much protein in a teen athlete's diet can harm health. Excess protein intake may lead to an increased risk of kidney stones, reduced bone mass density, and calcium imbalance. Inadequate water consumption and excess protein intake can increase the risk of dehydration. Excessive protein consumption can also put undue stress on the liver and kidneys, which are not fully developed in teens. A protein-rich diet can also lead to an unbalanced diet, as increased protein intake may reduce other essential nutrients, such as carbohydrates and fats, necessary for healthy growth and development.

Additionally, while protein is vital for building muscle mass, too much can cause GI distress in young athletes - so make sure your teen gets the right amount. Teen athletes should consume between 0.8g/kg -1.5g/kg of protein daily. How much they need can vary between training regimes and growth spurts.

Recording what is eaten and how much and comparing it to energy levels and emotional states will help pinpoint how much protein teen athletes need. Remember, though, their bodies are changing all the time, and one day they may need more protein than the last, so unfortunately, there aren't any definitive rules around protein consumption levels.

### TYPES OF FOODS VARY IN THEIR CALORIC CONTENT PER GRAM:

- **_Carbohydrates_** provide four calories per gram.
- **_Fats_** provide nine calories per gram.
- **_Proteins_** provide four calories per gram.

IF YOUR TEEN athlete needs about 2000 calories in one day, he can get there by consuming 500-600 grams of carbs (2000-2400 kcal) or 250-300 grams of protein and fat (2250 - 2700 kcal).

### ENERGY DENSITY OF FOODS

EMILY EDISON, MS, RD, CSSD, owner of Momentum Nutrition, explains, "Energy density is an important consideration when fueling for sport or training." High-volume sports like running can cause us to feel stuffed if we ignore energy density—the amount of food with the highest caloric content—so our stomachs don't get overloaded from too much volume. Energy-dense foods are vital in helping athletes meet their energy needs without feeling weighed down by all that food they'd have to eat otherwise; these foods can help build lean body mass. In short, energy density is an essential part of any athlete's nutrition plan and must be a consideration. (Kadey, 2022)

WHEN FEEDING A TEEN ATHLETE, you must know what types of food you should be providing and how much. To help you make the best decisions for your teen athlete, considering the energy density of macronutrients and the daily caloric needs of teen athletes can come in handy. The energy density of food refers to the amount of energy or calories contained in each weight or volume- usually per gram or ounce. Macronutrients are protein, carbohydrates, and fats – which all have different energy densities; proteins have the lowest energy density while fats have the highest. Knowing this information can help you manipulate the energy density of meals by adjusting portion sizes and ingredients with higher or lower caloric content accordingly.

FOR INSTANCE, if your teen athlete requires more calories for their activity level, you can add extra protein and fats to a meal to increase its energy density. On the other hand, if your teen's caloric needs are lower than usual, you can opt for foods with low energy density to reduce overall calorie intake without sacrificing portion size or hunger satisfaction.

BY UNDERSTANDING the concept of energy density and how it relates to macronutrient consumption, parents of teen athletes have an essential tool in helping their kids reach optimal performance levels while still having a healthy diet. By making wise and informed food choices, your youngster will be well on their way as they strive towards success.

MICRONUTRIENTS ARE vitamins and minerals essential for life and growth, such as calcium, magnesium, potassium, zinc, and iron. Teenage athletes need these micronutrients more than other teens. Their increased need is because they lose more micronutrients through sweating during physical activity. To ensure teen athletes get the proper micronutrients to keep them healthy and performing their best, include a variety of foods in the diet. Proteins, fats, and carbohydrates from various plant and animal sources will help ensure this.

## DAILY CALORIC NEED

AS A PARENT OF A TEEN ATHLETE, you know that proper nutrition is essential for your child's performance. Furthermore, figuring out daily caloric needs is also vital for optimal performance and health. The caloric requirements of teen athletes vary depending on their activity level and body size. Generally speaking, they should consume about 14-18 calories per pound (30-40 calories per kilogram) of their body weight each day. For example, an active teenage athlete who weighs 130 pounds would need around 1,820 - 2,340 calories daily to reach his peak performance in sports.

## FOOD LOG

THE FOOD LOG is an excellent tool for athletes of any level. It can help the athlete, and in turn, their parents or coach, see what kind of nutrition they need for optimal performance. Just look at Michael Phelps's 10000-calorie-a-day diet! Michael Phelps' nutritional intake of 10000 calories/day is extraordinary. However, his practice regimen demanded it. His daily routine included two four-hour practices and a one-hour weightlifting session. During this time, he did intense physical activity such as swimming, running, biking, and weight training. Given the sheer energy required to complete these tasks daily, it's no wonder his caloric needs were so high. As an athlete at the top of his game trying to maintain peak performance, Phelps had to ensure he was getting enough fuel to keep up with the demands of his sport. And while many people might think this is excessive or unhealthy, it is necessary for an elite-level athlete like him. Michael Phelps' extreme calorie intake exemplifies how much fuel one needs when putting in intense physical effort daily.

THE FOOD LOG can provide valuable information about the energy needed and the foods best suited for optimal performance. Tracking the intake will make assessing whether the athlete is getting enough nutrients and calories from their current diet easier. For example, if the teen athlete is not performing as well as expected in training or competitions, please use the food log to identify deficiencies and increase calorie intake appropriately. Understanding your teen athlete's caloric and nutritional needs is vital in helping them achieve their peak performance. Tracking their intake through a food log will provide essential information that can help ensure they get the right amount of energy and nutrients for optimal performance.

I HAVE CREATED a food log book, an excellent resource for teenage athletes, as it allows them to track and monitor their progress and stay motivated. It includes 120 days of tracking to record various metrics, including foods eaten, exercises completed, sleep hours achieved, and workouts performed. You and your athlete can use this information to assess current performance levels and develop future strategies to help reach the desired goals. The food log also provides an opportunity for self-reflection, allowing teen athletes to reflect on their habits and identify areas where they can improve food options to optimize performance. With this simple tool, teen athletes can stay on top of their physical health while achieving peak performance results.

## ORGANIC VS. NON-ORGANIC

PARENTS OF TEEN athletes can face a problematic debate between organic vs. non-organic food. Deciding which type is best for their child and their wallet can be overwhelming.

MANY BELIEVE organic foods have nutritional superiority over non-organic foods because they are free from artificial preservatives and harmful pesticides. Organic foods also tend to be fresher, as they don't contain additives that keep them shelf-stable for extended periods. Fresher food means that teens can get more vitamins and minerals from their food when eating organically since the nutrient quality of foods decays overtime on the grocery shelf.

FURTHERMORE, organic foods are not only healthier but also safer. Pesticides used in regular products can be a health hazard, so it's important to avoid them.

SOME OF THE Organic fruits and Vegetables you Should Opt for Due to High Pesticide Use in Non-Organic Types Include:

- *Strawberries*
- *Spinach Kale*
- *Mustard & collard greens*
- *Peaches*
- *Pears*
- *Nectarines*
- *Apples*
- *Grapes*
- *Bell and hot peppers*
- *Cherries*
- *Blueberries*
- *Green beans*
- *Celery*

THESE FOODS DON'T HAVE any peel or outer covering to protect the fruit from pesticide and herbicide contamination. Make sure to look for the organic label when shopping to ensure that you're getting the best quality products (GreenSmoothieGirl - Achieve Extraordinary Health!, 2018)

HOWEVER, not everyone can afford or find the higher price tag associated with organic foods available locally. Non-organic foods may be more accessible; the good news is that they still contain the same essential nutrients. Eating non-organic food has some drawbacks: it may contain pesticides or other chemicals that can have negative health implications over time. Just be sure to wash and rinse them thoroughly.

Plenty of Nutritious Options are Still Available when Shopping for Non-Organic Items Which Are Okay to Eat. They Include:

- _Avocados_
- _Pineapple_
- _Onions_
- _Papaya_
- _Sweet peas_
- _Asparagus_
- _Honeydew Melon_
- _Kiwi_
- _Cabbage_
- _Mushrooms_
- _Mangoes_
- _Sweet potatoes_
- _Watermelon_
- _Carrots_
- _Bananas_
- _Oranges_
- _Pumpkins_

Both organic and non-organic foods have their pros and cons. Parents should consider what's available to them regarding price, availability, and any potential health benefits when deciding on their food choices for athletes. Either way, choosing fresh fruits and vegetables whenever possible is essential – whether organic or not. (M. J. Brown & (uk), 2021) However, some canned and flash-frozen fruits and vegetables can contain the same nutrients depending on the packing process.

## GRASS FED VS. GRAIN FED

WHEN IT COMES to feeding your teen athlete, one of the biggest debates is between grass-fed and grain-fed meats. While both can provide significant nutritional benefits, there are several factors to consider when making the decision. Studies show that grass-fed beef is typically higher in total nutrients, phytonutrients, antioxidants, vital fatty acids, vita- mins, minerals, protein, and amino acids than grain-fed beef. Grain-fed foods, on the other hand, are generally more affordable and easier to find. Ultimately, there is yet to be a definitive answer regarding choosing between grass-fed vs. grain-fed food for teen athletes. The best option will vary depending on the athlete's budget, taste preferences, and dietary needs. (Grass-Fed Beef: Is It Good for You?, n.d.)

## RAW VS. COOKED FOOD

RAW VERSUS COOKED food is a classic debate that athletes often face. Both options have advantages and drawbacks. Raw foods are generally higher in nutrients than cooked foods since they are not exposed to high temperatures, which can take essential nutrients away. Raw fruits and veggies also offer plenty of fiber necessary for healthy digestion. On top of that, many believe that consuming raw natural foods helps reduce inflammation levels throughout the body.

ON THE OTHER HAND, cooked foods offer a few advantages. Generally, the cooking process breaks down tough fiber and makes certain nutrients more bioavailable - meaning teens can absorb them better than when they are raw. Additionally, roasting or sautéing veggies can make them taste better for picky eaters, while boiling reduces the naturally occurring toxins in some items like potatoes and beans.

It's best to stick with a varied diet that includes both raw and cooked options - this way, teens benefit from each. Encourage your teen athlete to mix up their meals throughout the week, watching for balanced combinations of carbs, protein, and healthy fats on their plate. That way, they'll get all the nutrients they need to perform at their best and stay safe on the field. (Muinos, 2011)

## FOODS YOUR ATHLETE SHOULD AVOID

WHEN PROVIDING Athletes with the Necessary Calories and Nutrients, Avoid these Foods for Peak Performance. Avoid:

- *Processed meats* like hot dogs and bacon
- *Sugary foods* like donuts and candy
- *Pre-packaged* meals and snacks
- *Sugary sports drinks* and juices
- *Diet soda*
- *White bread*
- *Flavored yogurts*
- *Bottled salad dressings*

NOT ONLY DO these foods lack nutritional value, but they can also harm training or game-day performance.

ADDITIONALLY, Athletes Should Avoid these Common Additives:

- *Monosodium Glutamate*
- *High Fructose Corn Syrup*
- *Artificial sweeteners* (Sucralose, saccharine, and aspartame)
- *Nitrates* (sodium nitrate and monopotassium glutamate)

EATING these common additives can lead to fatigue, headache, and lack of energy which may hinder a teen athlete's performance. Therefore, parents of teen athletes must watch what their teens eat to remain at the top of their game and be diligent about reading food labels.

FAST FOOD IS another culprit that teenage athletes should avoid. These meals may seem convenient for busy athletes, but they contain many empty calories from fat, sugar, and salt with minimal nutritional value. Eating a lot of fast food can also cause teens to become dependent on it later in life when, in fact, they should be eating healthy to establish positive habits.

FINALLY, sugary drinks, such as sodas and energy drinks, are not recommended for teen athletes. These beverages contain high amounts of sugar and added chemicals that can increase the risk of becoming overweight or obese. Additionally, they provide minimal nutritional benefits and can lead to dehydration. (Follow the Athlete Diet, n.d.)

## HOME-MADE VS. STORE-BOUGHT

AS PARENTS, ensuring our teenage athletes consume nutritious meals is a top priority for both their physical AND mental health. But with busy schedules and time constraints, it can be difficult to provide healthy meals that energize them for their sports activities. The good news is that you don't need to settle for store-bought pre-packaged foods when it comes to feeding your teen athlete. Home-cooked meals offer far more nutritional value than store bought and are just as convenient. Home-made meals can provide the needed energy boost and replenishment for muscle growth in young athletes.

GET your athlete involved in the kitchen - planning meals, shopping for ingredients, and preparing nutritious meals can be pleasurable. Everyone can benefit from teaching them valuable cooking skills that will last a lifetime. You'll gain more cooks for the kitchen, and they'll learn some practical adult skills. I'm sure I'm not alone when I say that store-bought bread can sometimes be disappointing. It's often full of unhealthy ingredients, artificial flavors, and preservatives. That's why I decided to take matters into my own hands and start baking our bread. With just a few ingredients like non-bleached whole wheat flour, yeast, organic butter, water, milk, and a pinch of Himalayan salt (and a little honey for sweetness), I could make something much healthier than anything we could buy in the store - while tasting significantly better too. To make life easier on myself (and anyone who wants to give home baking a go), I usually made a couple of loaves on Sundays to last us throughout the week. Making home-cooked meals ensures your teen athlete gets the best nutrition possible – so it's a win- win.

## Healthy Snacking

FOR TEENAGE ATHLETES, healthy snacks are a great way to keep their energy levels up and fuel their bodies with the necessary nutrients. Eating balanced snacks between meals or before and after physical activity can help maintain an optimal level of performance Regarding snacking, think natural, nutrient-dense foods like fruits, vegetables, nuts and seeds, whole grains, nutritional bars, dairy products like yogurt or cottage cheese, or high- protein smoothies. These can provide an essential source of carbohydrates that will give you sustained energy during your activities and vitamins and minerals that support healthy growth and development.

## Foods for Improved Immune Function and Healing

CERTAIN FOODS CAN PROVIDE the energy teen athletes need, help improve their immune system, and aid in healing after a challenging game or workout.

IF YOU HAVE a teen athlete in your life, stock up on these super-foods to give them an extra edge:

- *Citrus fruits like oranges or grapefruits Red bell peppers*
- *Broccoli and other cruciferous vegetables Garlic*
- *Ginger*
- *Dark green leafy vegetables Eggs*
- *Salmon*
- *Berries of all kinds Yogurt (especially Greek)*
- *Nuts and seeds such as almonds, walnuts, flaxseeds, and chia seeds*
- *Turmeric, which is a spice and can be a tea Green Tea*
- *Papaya*
- *Kiwi*
- *Poultry such as chicken or turkey*
- *Shellfish like shrimp, scallops, oysters, and crabs*
- *Sweet potatoes* (Cassandra Calabrese, 2022)

THESE FOODS ARE easy to incorporate into a balanced diet for your teen athlete and can give them a healthy boost with these nutrient-packed meals.

## MICROWAVING FOOD

THE MICROWAVE IS one of the best cooking solutions- hands down. With everything happening in your teen's hectic busy life, from homework to extracurriculars, you want them to eat healthy and safe food. It is common to make healthy foods over the weekend for consumption during the week. A casserole cooked during the weekend can be consumed all week with minimal effort. Just cut a piece and reheat. Rest assured, with some basic knowledge and tips about microwave cooking, you can confidently ensure your teen athlete gets the nourishment they need without sacrificing their safety.

ONE COMMON CONCERN about microwaves is radiation exposure. While it may seem like something straight out of a science fiction movie, it's important to note that radiation emitted by microwaves is non-ionizing and not known to cause any harm. When used correctly (and not tampered with), microwaves are one of the safest and most efficient methods of cooking food.

WHEN PREPARING food in the microwave, make sure to choose cookware approved for microwave use, as some materials can't withstand high temperatures and may contain toxins that could leech into your teen's food. Acceptable cookware is glass, paper, and porcelain. Avoid plastic, Styrofoam, and most to-go containers. Also, always remember to use a lid when possible; this will help keep moisture and heat in while preventing bacteria from entering the food. I use a wet paper towel to cover my food, which prevents foods from drying out and protects the inside of my microwave from food spatter. Finally, thoroughly clean any utensils or dishes used in the process - microwaving doesn't mean it's okay to slack off on hygiene. With these essential tips, you can rest easy knowing your teen athlete is getting healthy meals cooked safely and deliciously in no time. (J. Brown, 2020)

# 5

## NUTRITIONAL NEEDS BY SPORT & GENDER

I t's no secret that teens have big appetites. But if your child is an athlete, they need even more nutrition than the average teenager. That's why it's vital to understand teen athletes' unique nutritional needs for optimal performance. Like building a house, the "building materials" for a healthy diet should tailor to teen athletes to ensure they can access all the necessary nutrients and vitamins to reach their goals. Meanwhile, too much of a particular nutrient can cause just as many problems as not enough. Parents of teen athletes must understand what macronutrient and micronutrient portions are right for their teen athletes to build a strong body and healthy mind. Reviewing the nutrient and caloric needs of teens of different ages, genders, and sports requirements is vital for ensuring your athlete is eating and drinking enough for optimal health, including a guide with the proper ways of gaining or losing weight for an optimally fit body.

## Nutritional Needs by Gender, Age, Development, and Sport

EVERY SPORT REQUIRES a different level of energy and nutrition, from soccer to swimming and gymnastics, for optimal performance. Ensuring your teen gets the right amount and type of fuel depends on age, gender, development stage, and sport- specific requirements. Here is the essential information to ensure your teen gets enough calories, protein, vitamins, minerals, carbohydrates, and fats for peak performance in their chosen sport.

## Nutritional Needs by Sport

PHYSICAL INTENSITY PLAYS a vital role in understanding the nutritional needs of any athlete. Knowing which sports are more intense than others is essential. With so many sports to play, it takes time to determine what those needs should be.

KNOWING the level of physical intensity in your teen's chosen sport can help you better understand their nutritional needs and ensure they reach peak performance. (Classification of Physical Activity and Level of Intensity, n.d.) Low-intensity sports like golf and bowling require fewer calories than moderate-intensity activities like cycling or tennis. But don't forget, most teenage golfers walk the course instead of riding in a cart, so packing a healthy snack like a protein bar isn't out of the question. Additionally, these sports often only require carbohydrate replacement drinks for energy if they last longer than 30 minutes. On the other hand, high-intensity sports like basketball and hockey will require more calories before training and competition, if possible, because they involve maximum effort for long periods. Athletes need snacks or meals containing carbohydrates and proteins to replenish energy, stabilize their blood sugar, and repair their muscles.

HERE'S a quick rundown of some common sports and where they fall on the physical intensity scale:

- _Low-Intensity Sports_: Golf, Bowling, Table Tennis
- _Moderate-Intensity Sports_: Volleyball, Cycling (depending on the event), Football
- _High-Intensity Sports:_ Soccer, Basketball, Tennis, Swimming

JUST REMEMBER THE HIGHER INTENSITY, the more quality calories the athlete needs.

## NUTRITIONAL NEEDS BY AGE & GENDER

HERE'S a breakdown of estimated calorie requirements by age, gender, and activity level for teenage athletes.

- _Active teen boys_ typically need 3,000-4000 calories daily.
- _Active teen girls_ need 2,000-3,000 calories per day.

OUR DAUGHTER'S LIFE, during her high school and club swimming career, revolved around four things: swimming, sleeping, eating, and school work. Our job was to make sure there were plenty of good food choices to keep her fueled up. Additionally, as the sports performance and nutrition counselor for the San Diego Women's Swim and Dive team, I constantly had to reinforce the need for good, quality calories to both the coaches and the swimmers.

THERE ARE a few things to remember regarding individualized caloric needs. While teens need more calories than younger children or adults due to their growth, they don't necessarily need more energy if they are inactive. Overeating can lead to unhealthy weight gain and other dietary issues, so teen athletes must get the right fuel. (Purcell & Canadian Pediatric Society, Pediatric Sports, and Exercise Medicine Section, 2013)

## BREAKDOWN OF MACRONUTRIENTS AND MICRONUTRIENTS

HERE'S a breakdown of what macronutrients and micronutrients your teen should eat for optimum performance:

- *Carbohydrates* are an essential energy source for the body, especially during physical activity. Teen athletes should aim to consume 45-65% of their calories from carbohydrates such as grains, fruits, vegetables, nuts, legumes, and dairy products.
- *Protein* plays a significant role in muscle growth and repair after intense activity. Your teen needs 1.2-1.7 grams of protein per kilogram (0.5-0.8 g/lb) of body

weight per day to build muscle mass and prevent fatigue. Good protein sources include meat, fish, eggs, dairy products, nuts, and seeds. Power sports like football, weightlifting, gymnastics, and wrestling require 1.0-1.5 g/kg/day.

- *Fats* are essential to a teenager's diet as they provide energy for activity and help the body absorb vitamins. Aim for 20-35% of total calories from fats such as vegetable oils (canola oil, olive oil), nuts and seeds, fish oils (salmon), avocados, and nut butter.

MICRONUTRIENTS such as vitamins and minerals are also essential for an athlete's health and performance. Foods rich in micronutrients include fruits, vegetables, whole grains, legumes, nuts, and seeds - all of which should be part of your teen athlete's diet.

## KEEPING SCORE

TRACKING NUTRITION, physical activity, and sleep are all essential for any player, but even more so for teens who are still developing. You'll get an accurate picture of their overall health by tracking what your teen is eating, how much exercise they're getting each day, and how well they're sleeping at night regularly. Not only will these records help ensure that your teen is meeting their nutritional needs and staying active enough to keep in shape, but they will also provide a valuable source of information should any injuries occur. With an up-to-date record of what your teen is eating, drinking, and how much exercise they're getting, you can quickly pinpoint any underlying health issues that may have contributed to the injury.

KEEPING score records can also help prevent burnout and reduce stress among teen athletes. By tracking their performance over time, you'll be able to identify when they are overexerting themselves or showing signs of fatigue — red flags that can indicate the need for better rest or recovery strategies.

THE NEXT CHAPTER will focus on how teenage athletes can create a healthy diet with all the necessary nutrients. Furthermore, it will also discuss how an athlete's nutrition needs can change as they go through different phases of growth and development.

# 6

---

## ENCOURAGE HEALTHY EATING HABITS

F ood plays a vital role in all our lives, especially for athletes. It influences how we feel, act, and perform on the field—and beyond. That's why having a healthy relationship with food is so important. A healthy relationship with food starts by recognizing that there's more than one way to eat healthily. Your teen athlete doesn't have to follow any one diet or eliminate certain foods completely; instead, they should experiment and find out what works best for them. By creating an environment where they can explore different foods and learn to recognize their body's signals, you can help them develop a healthy attitude toward food.

As a PARENT OF A TEEN ATHLETE, you must encourage your teen to think about food as their friend and fuel-not the enemy or some mystical force that evades them. After all, what's the point of training for hours if you don't have the proper nutrition to help you reach peak performance? Eating healthy food is just as important as exercising to boost athletic performance. Ensure your teen knows that eating well isn't just "good" - it's great. Explain eating well will give them the energy and vigor they need to take on any physical, academic, and emotional challenges that come their way. Plus, they'll enjoy the added benefit of feeling great inside and out.

PARENTS SIGNIFICANTLY INFLUENCE how their children view food and body image, even if they don't realize it. Your teen is looking to you for cues about how to feel about their body size or shape. Will they see someone who loves and accepts them as they are? Are they seeing you enjoy eating healthy foods or turning away from all but "safe" foods? Do you have a positive relationship with food? Your teen may not be aware of the messages they're getting from you, but these unspoken queues can be powerful indicators of how to handle their self-image. It's essential to be mindful of what you say and how you act around food and body image. This doesn't mean you need to perform, but rather, take the time to demonstrate healthy behaviors concerning your body and diet. You can start by showing your teen, through example, that everyone is different and unique – including their bodies. Teach them that they don't need to fit into any fashion of beauty or body style; it's ok to be comfortable in their skin. By being a role model for healthy eating habits, positive self-image, and self-acceptance, you can equip your teen with skills that will last them a lifetime. Don't underestimate your influence on your teen's relationship with food and body image. It has the potential to make a big difference. (Developing Positive Attitudes Toward Food, n.d.)

## CREATING HEALTHY EATING HABITS AND A POSITIVE RELATIONSHIP WITH EXERCISE

WE ALL NEED an environment of balance. Teens can be hard on themselves regarding their body image and exercise routine. Help them recognize that everyone's body is different, and they don't always have to be "perfect" for their health goals to be successful. Set realistic expectations that are both achievable and sustainable.

SET LIMITS. It's essential to monitor how much time your teen spends on physical activity and practice and how much rest they get each day. Too little rest or too much exercise can lead to overtraining syndrome, a condition where the body wears down due to excessive exercise. Setting healthy boundaries around their time can help them maintain a healthy weight.

### RESTRICT SWEETENED BEVERAGES

SUGARY DRINKS ARE OFTEN empty calories that can add up quickly and contribute to unhealthy weight gain for young athletes. Stick with water, whole milk, and other nutritious options while limiting sodas and fruit juices when possible. Or cut the juice with water- half water, half juice.

## USE POSITIVE MESSAGES

AVOID COMPARING your athlete to other athletes and their bodies or commenting on their physical appearance. Instead, use positive language and messages emphasizing effort and improvement rather than perfection.

## DON'T USE FOOD AS A REWARD.

FOOD CAN BE an easy way to show appreciation, but focusing on non-food rewards such as special activities or quality time together is essential. This will help your teen athlete form positive habits around eating and maintaining a healthy weight.

## PLAN, SHOP, AND COOK HEALTHY MEALS

IT'S NOT ALWAYS easy for teens to make good dietary decisions when they are out with friends or away on trips, so having healthy options available at home is critical. Spend time planning for meals by shopping for nutritious ingredients and trying new recipes together. Your athlete WILL need to know how to cook for themselves at some point in their lives! Sundays were reserved for a day of rest and for prepping our meals for the upcoming week. We got creative with making healthy snacks we could take on the go, from trail mix and quiches to casseroles and baked sweet potatoes. This way, no matter how hectic our everyday lives became, we always had easy access to nutritious food. The effort put in on Sunday made it possible to enjoy more relaxed days during the week.

To this day, I still make time for some Sunday meal prep – it's become a habit that helps me maintain my energy while juggling all my daily tasks.

## AVOID FEEDING OVERSIZED PORTIONS

MANY PARENTS and coaches unknowingly encourage unhealthy weight gain in teen athletes by providing oversized portions or pressure to "clean their plate" at mealtimes. Instead, let your teen athlete judge how much they need to eat and keep portion sizes reasonable.

## TEACH YOUR TEEN ABOUT HUNGER AND FULLNESS CUES

EATING BASED on cravings or external cues can lead to overeating which can cause an increase in weight over time. Help your teen athlete become more aware of their internal hunger and satiety signals to make better decisions around food intake. Additionally, help them identify triggers that may cause them to overeat, like stress and fatigue. Many times instead of being hungry we are actually dehydrated.

## DEVELOP CRITICAL THINKING SKILLS

THE MEDIA often presents unrealistic images and expectations regarding body image and dieting. Teach your teen to be critical of these messages and cultivate an attitude of self-acceptance and appreciation. Please encourage them to challenge peer pressure by being confident in their own skin.

## HEALTHY WEIGHT MANAGEMENT: GAIN AND LOSS DONE RIGHT

IT'S no secret that maintaining a healthy weight is essential for everyone, but especially for teenage athletes. In the world of sports, there are many tempting shortcuts like quick-fix diets and fad fitness regimes that promise drastic results in little time - these diets can be hazardous. Rapid weight gain or loss can have serious long-term health consequences and even put your athletic performance at risk. I had a friend in high school on the wrestling team; on competition days, he wore multiple layers and a trash bag with the neck and arms cut out to "sweat his way to his weight class." Additionally, he would spit into a cup all day to try to lose any additional "water weight." Not only was his behavior what I considered gross, but it was also unhealthy.

## TIPS AND STRATEGIES FOR HEALTHY WEIGHT GAIN

I KNOW GETTING your teens to eat enough can be hard when they're busy with sports and other activities. But to increase weight and muscle mass healthily, they will likely need to increase their caloric intake.

FOLLOW THESE GUIDELINES FOR HEALTHY WEIGHT GAIN:

- *Eat enough Calories to Encourage Muscle Growth*. As mentioned, a good rule of thumb regarding calorie intake for teen athletes is anywhere from 2000-3000 per day, depending on their activity level. If their activity level is high, don't be afraid to up their caloric intake. Ensure they get adequate protein in their diet – around 1 gram per pound of body weight or even more if they want to build muscle mass noticeably. They may need to eat more frequently, so having healthy, well-rounded meals and snacks may be necessary.
- *Weight Training*. Ensure your teen athlete does resistance training, such as weightlifting or bodyweight exercises. Strength training will help to build muscle and can also help with overall physical performance.
- *Stay Consistent*. All aspects of their fitness routine – nutrition, exercise, sleep, and recovery- must stay consistent. These are all critical components in achieving healthy weight gain and will be essential for optimal performance.

TIPS AND STRATEGIES FOR HEALTHY WEIGHT LOSS

WEIGHT LOSS CAN BE tricky for teens, especially when competing in competitive sports. It's possible to help your teen athlete stay fit and active while getting the proper nutrition for peak performance.

FOLLOW THESE GUIDELINES FOR HEALTHY WEIGHT LOSS:

*ENCOURAGE SMART SNACKING.* Having access to nutrient- dense snacks like fruits, vegetables, string cheese, nuts, etc., can help keep energy levels up during the day. Try packing pre-cut, single-serve bags of snacks that your teen can quickly grab before they head out the door. Making trail mix was an essential part of our family's grocery list—not only because it was a healthy and nutritious snack but also because it was relatively affordable. I would scour the supermarket shelves to find sunflower seeds, pepitas, raisins, and organic dark chocolate chips that fit within our budget. After mixing everything in a bowl, I would then portion individual servings into snack-sized bags, ensuring each of us had their supply of trail mix for on-the-go snacking. This way, we always had a handy supply of nourishment with us wherever we went. Plus, since I am allergic to most nuts found in commercial mixtures, home-made trail mix allowed me to enjoy snacking safely. All in all, making our trail mix was a win-win for everyone— good for us and good for the budget. It gave my kids an intelligent snacking option, which was a healthier option.

- *Set a Good Example.* Remember that your teen will learn from what you do, so be sure to model healthy lifestyle behaviors like eating nutritious meals and exercising regularly. If you're planning an afternoon of sports watching and snacking, demonstrate healthy habits by exercising before the afternoon and adding some healthy snacks like hummus and carrots.
- *Limit Sugary Drinks*. Sugary sodas, juices, and sports drinks can contribute to weight gain. Encourage your teen to drink more water instead. Or try cutting

juices with water so they are one-half water and one-half juice.

- *Talk about Food Openly*. Discussing nutrition as a family is a great way to reinforce healthy habits and keep everyone accountable. Creating accountability will help ensure that your teen has access to balanced meals designed for optimal performance in their sport of choice.
- *Stay away from Fad Diets and Shortcuts*. Fad diets may seem easy to lose weight quickly, but they're often ineffective and potentially dangerous for teen athletes. Instead of relying on these trendy approaches, please encourage them to adopt healthy habits that last a lifetime.
- *Encourage Nutrient-Dense Foods*. Ensure your teenager gets enough calories by choosing nutrient-dense foods like vegetables, fruits, whole grains, lean proteins, and healthy fats. These will give them the energy they need without packing on extra pounds.
- *Focus on Performance, not Weight*. While it is crucial to maintain a healthy weight, your teen athlete should never feel like a number on the scale determines their worth. Please encourage them to focus on performance goals rather than what the scale says.
- *Offer Support*. As a parent, you know your teenager best and are likely aware of any underlying pressures or issues contributing to weight gain. Support without judgment is vital in helping them through any difficult times they may be facing.

BY IMPLEMENTING THESE TIPS, parents can help their teen athletes maintain a healthy weight without sacrificing performance or self-esteem. With proper guidance, teens can have a positive experience with sports while learning to make good nutrition and physical activity decisions. (Advice for Parents of Healthy-Weight Children, n.d.)

UNDERSTANDING the nutritional needs and the emotional connection to food can help us, as parents, steer our children in the direction of creating a healthy relationship with food. Try implementing some of the tips like meal planning or healthy snack creation this week and see what a difference it can make for your family in general and your athlete.

THE NEXT CHAPTER will enable you to recognize when the relationship your athlete has with food takes a turn for the worst. The information found therein may someday save the life of your child. Yes, the issue is that BIG.

## 7

## THE DANGERS OF DIETING AND
## DISORDERED EATING IN ATHLETES

E ATING disorders are a severe issue for teen athletes that must be addressed to ensure their safety and well-being. "Disordered eating" is an umbrella term that describes any abnormal behavior related to food or body image, such as extreme dieting, binge eating, skipping meals, overexercising, or excessive calorie counting. While disordered eating isn't necessarily an eating disorder (ED), it can be a gateway to full-blown Eds like anorexia nervosa or bulimia nervosa.

ATHLETES ARE PARTICULARLY at risk for developing eating disorders because they may feel pressure from coaches and teammates to achieve unrealistic body standards. Common eating disorders include anorexia nervosa and other forms of restrictive eating, bulimia nervosa and other forms of binge/purge behaviors, orthorexia (an obsession with healthy eating), muscle dysmorphia (a distorted body image in which athletes view themselves as too small despite being muscular), and compulsive exercise.

THE EFFECTS of eating disorders on teen athletes can be physically and emotionally devastating. In addition to the physical health risks associated with eating disorders- such as weakened bones, dehydration, organ failure, and electrolyte imbalances-eating disorders can also cause mental health issues like depression or anxiety. You can see how this can become a vicious cycle by understanding the connection between nutrition and mental health. If left untreated, eating disorders can lead to death.

THE MOST AT-RISK athletes for developing an eating disorder are highly competitive or driven by perfectionism- Additionally, studies show that sports that emphasize body image such as gymnastics and figure skating have higher levels of eating issues. You should be familiar with the warning signs of distorted eating habits.

LOOK FOR THESE WARNING SIGNS:

- *Extreme weight loss or gain*
- *Drastic fluctuations in performance*
- *Difficulty sleeping*
- *Avoiding meals with teammates or family members*
- *Spending excessive amounts of time working out*
- *An obsession with their diet or body image*
- *Eliminating food groups or trying new "diets"*

IF YOU NOTICE any of these signs in your teenage athlete, acting immediately by speaking to a medical professional or mental health expert is essential. I have a friend who struggled with bulimia in her teen and early adult years; her disorder was brought to light by her dentist, who noticed the enamel on her teeth was too thin because of the bile from when she made herself throw up. No one in her family had suspected anything was wrong.

EATING disorders are a real and serious issue, particularly in teen athletes. By recognizing the warning signs and intervening early, you can provide your teen athlete with the support they need to stay physically and mentally healthy. (Bushell, 2022) If left untreated, eating disorders can be dangerous for your teen. Taking proactive steps to prevent eating disorders is essential for the well-being of teen athletes. Early intervention can address disordered eating behaviors before they become full-blown eating disorders. Educating teens about proper nutrition, creating an encouraging environment where body diversity is celebrated, and providing mental health support when needed are all necessary measures parents and coaches should take to protect teen athletes from developing eating disorders.

## EATING DISORDERS IN BOTH MALE AND FEMALE ATHLETES

EATING disorders should never be disregarded or overlooked, regardless of gender. Although the figures for male teen athletes suffering from eating disorders are much lower than those for female athletes, it is essential to note that this issue can affect males too. According to research published in Sports Medicine, approximately 4-13% of male athletes have reported having an eating disorder. Of these cases, the most affected sports were wrestling and swimming; however, other sports, such as gymnastics and rowing, also had a high rate of occurrences. It is essential to acknowledge the prevalence of this issue among male and female athletes and provide appropriate resources for both genders.

TYPES OF EATING DISORDERS:

- *Anorexia* is characterized by extreme restriction of food intake to the point of unhealthy weight loss and a distorted perception of body image. Signs may include a drastic reduction in calorie intake, avoidance of social meals or activities involving food, excessive exercise, and frequent weigh-ins.
- *Bulimia* is quickly consuming large amounts of food, followed by purging through vomiting or laxative use. Symptoms often manifest themselves as secretive episodes of binging and purging accompanied by feelings of guilt and shame.
- *Binge-Eating Disorder* is uncontrollable overeating episodes involving no purging afterward. Signs include eating large quantities of food in a short period, feeling unable to control one's eating habits, and often, feelings of guilt and distress after eating binges.

COMPULSIVE EXERCISE IS one of the classic symptoms of ANY of these types of body image disorder. Teen athletes may feel driven to push themselves harder than ever before, leading to over-exercising or even avoiding rest days altogether. This behavior can eventually cause physical exhaustion and a decline in performance.

ALTHOUGH NO SINGLE factor is identified as causing eating disorders in teen athletes, several predisposing factors can put them at risk. These include body image issues, stress from competition, and social pressures from teammates or coaches. Social media can harm your athlete's overall mental health, especially when comparing themselves to other athletes, models, etc. Furthermore, social media may expose your athlete to cyber-bullying, leading to an eating disorder or other mental health challenges.

EATING disorders in teen athletes can also lead to several medical complications. These include electrolyte imbalances, cardiac abnormalities, weakened bones, and muscles, and an increased risk for mental health problems. When diagnosing athletes with eating disorders, it is crucial to consider their unique circumstances. Clinicians should consider the athlete's age, gender, performance level, and behavior patterns when diagnosing.

TREATMENT OPTIONS for teen athletes with eating disorders vary depending on the individual. They involve psychotherapy sessions along with nutritional counseling and physical activity modifications. In severe cases, medications may be prescribed to help manage symptoms, or in-resident treatment stays may be necessary. All these measures are designed to help teen athletes achieve a healthy life balance.

ULTIMATELY, it is essential to recognize the signs of eating disorders in teen athletes and take steps to address them as soon as possible. With the proper support and treatment, these young athletes can get back on track and continue pursuing their dreams. (Website, n.d.)

## SUPPORT YOUR TEEN ATHLETE

AS PARENTS, it can be heart-breaking watching our teens face challenges. But sometimes, those challenges are what they need to grow and learn important life lessons. Here are a few tips for helping your teen navigate the tricky waters of growing up:

- *Be Patient*: Parenting teenagers can be a roller-coaster of emotions. So don't expect to get it right every time. Remember that your teen is probably more sensitive and emotional than adults around them, so try not to be too hard on them if they make mistakes.
- *Talk to Them:* Granted, teens are not the best communicators. However, open communication between you and your child is the key to supporting them through any challenge, including eating disorders. Find out what they're struggling with and listen without judgment or criticism. Show interest in the issues they're facing, which will help your teen feel supported by you and encourage them to open up more in the future.
- *Voice your Unconditional Love:* Eating disorders can be overwhelming, and your teen may feel like they don't have control over the situation. By reassuring them that your love for them is unconditional, you're helping provide comfort and security.

- *Educate Yourself on Eating Disorders:* Learning about an eating disorder's signs, symptoms, treatments, and causes will help you better understand what your child is going through. It will also make it easier to recognize if their condition worsens or if they need extra support from a health professional.

- *Accompany your Teen to their Appointments:* Whether with a doctor or psychologist, attending an appointment with your child can benefit both of you if your teen is comfortable with you being in the meeting. Not only will it allow you to be in the loop, but you'll also be able to ask questions and get involved in their treatment plan.

- *Provide Support with School Work:* Eating disorders can affect a child's academic performance, as well as their athletic performance, so that they may need extra help with their studies. Helping with additional tutoring or guidance with assignments can make a massive difference in helping your teen stay on top of their schoolwork throughout this challenging time. Pressure to perform in all areas of their lives can be overwhelming for teens; communication with your teen athlete's school counselor to get additional time on assignments, modified tests, etc, may be necessary. That conversation should be 100% confidential with the school counselor.

- *Monitor your Teen's Overall Health:*In addition to providing emotional support, you should monitor any physical changes caused by an eating disorder, such as weight loss or difficulty sleeping. Keeping track of these changes allows you to adjust your child's treatment plan and alert their healthcare provider if necessary.

- *Join an Eating Disorders Support Group*: Being part of a support group can help you feel more connected to others going through similar experiences with their teens. It will also provide a safe environment to discuss concerns and find solutions.

- *Resolve to Spend More Time with Your Teen*: Spending quality time as a family is critical, especially during difficult times. Set aside some special one-on-one activities for the two of you, or plan fun outings with the whole family on weekends or holidays.

- *Keep an Eye on Your Other Children*: Eating disorders can be contagious, not like a flu but with behaviors, among siblings, so you must be aware of changes in your other children's behavior. If you notice any signs of an eating disorder, talk to them about it and seek help from a professional as soon as possible.

- *An Eating Disorder is NOT Chicken Pox or the Flu:* Eating disorders are mental health conditions with serious physical consequences if left untreated. It's important to remember that they don't just go away on their own and require treatment, support, and understanding for your child to recover from them. (Eating Disorders: About More than Food, n.d.)

EATING healthy is essential for teen athletes to perform at their best and stay fit. Furthermore, keeping track of weight gain or loss and recognizing potential eating disorders in your teen athlete is vital to creating a healthy relationship with food and exercise.

# 8

## LEVERAGING NUTRITION SUPPORT

This Chapter should be titled "Welcome to the Wild World of Sports Performance and Nutrition." The annual revenue in the United States for the sports nutrition and supplement market is over 44 BILLION dollars US. (Statista- the Statistics Portal, n.d.) That's A LOT of advertising dollars spent trying to entice you to buy their products. Consequently, as a parent of a teen athlete, it can feel like navigating an obstacle course when trying to figure out the best way to nourish your child. From sports drinks and protein shakes to supplements and food-tracking apps, there are so many options available that it's enough to make even the most experienced parents pull their hair out. This chapter is here to help you make sense of it all. We'll explore the pros and cons of various products on the market, giving you a better understanding of what works for your teen athlete's needs—with our insight, empowering you with the tools needed to make informed decisions about nutrition support.

IF YOU'RE a parent of a teenage athlete, there's no doubt you've heard the debate: is it better to focus on getting your teen the best sports nutrition or provide them with more traditional foods? On one side, some swear by protein shakes and energy supplements. But then again, some insist that real food provides all the fuel an athlete needs. For parents of teen athletes especially, it's essential to stay informed about what your kids are putting into their bodies so that they can perform at peak levels without sacrificing their health or safety. But remember-- just because something is marketed towards athletes doesn't mean it's healthy.

DETERMINING what approach is right for your teen athlete can be tricky. That's why this chapter will explore both sides of the debate so you can make an informed decision. We'll examine the benefits and drawbacks of focusing on sports nutrition and relying on wholesome meals made from natural ingredients. With this information, you'll be better equipped to decide which approach is best for your teen athlete.

## WATER VS. SPORTS DRINKS: THE GREAT DEBATE

THERE'S MORE to consider regarding hydration than what type of Gatorade (shudder) your athlete should have. Here are the pros and cons of water so you can make informed decisions about proper hydration for your child.

PROS OF WATER:

- *It's free or low-cost*
- *No added sugar or artificial ingredients*
- *Hydrates without adding calories*
- *Could improve skin health*
- *Natural thirst quencher*
- *Aids in digestion*
- *Supports healthy kidney function*
- *Reduces fatigue*
- *Helps prevent dehydration*
- *Lowers risk of developing kidney stones*

CONS OF WATER:

- Some water sources may contain *harmful bacteria*
- *Chlorine and other contaminants* could be an issue in some areas
- *Not enough electrolytes* to replace what is lost when exercising intensely over a long period
- *Not as flavorful* as other options, making it less enjoyable to drink for some people

THE NITTY-GRITTY OF SPORTS DRINKS

UNSURPRISINGLY, massive advertising campaigns have made sports drinks trendy among teen athletes. After all, they offer a compelling promise: "Rehydrate faster and recover quicker!" Unfortunately, the research isn't quite so straightforward.

While evidence suggests that sports drinks can help with rehydration, some dodgy figures indicate otherwise.

THE REALITY IS the amount of sugar in many sports drinks can do more harm than good regarding hydration. High levels of glucose, fructose, or any other sugar (sugars end in -ose when looking at food labels) found in these drinks can slow down your body's absorption of fluids, so the hydration boost may not be as expected. Plus, long-term consumption of sugary beverages increases the risk of obesity and dental caries. And while some sports drinks contain electrolytes, these don't necessarily make up for the water and nutrients lost during exercise. They can sometimes cause an imbalance in your body's natural electrolyte levels.

## BEWARE OF THE INGREDIENTS

SPORTS DRINKS ARE a great way to keep hydrated during activities, but there are some essential things to consider when choosing the right one. The main ingredients in most sports drinks are sugar, electrolytes, water, and sometimes flavoring or other additives.

SUGAR IS an essential source of energy during exercise and helps replenish lost carbohydrates as well as supplies power for muscles. However, too much-added sugar can be bad for your teen athlete's health in the long run since it contributes to weight gain and tooth decay. If you're looking for a healthier option, look out for sports drinks with naturally occurring sugars like glucose or fructose instead of added sweeteners like corn syrup or high-fructose corn syrup.

ELECTROLYTES ARE minerals that help maintain the water balance in our bodies and keep us hydrated, which is why they are vital ingredients in sports drinks. The most common electrolytes found in sports drinks are sodium, potassium, and calcium.

HOWEVER, it's also important to be aware of the other ingredients included in the drink. Some sports drinks contain artificial flavorings or additives like colors, preservatives, and caffeine that can be harmful if consumed in large amounts.

IN SHORT, when opting for a sports drink for your teen athletes, please read the labels carefully to know precisely the types of sugar, chemicals, and other additives you're putting into their bodies. Look for ones with natural sugars; fewer added fillers, and no artificial ingredients – all of which will keep your teen athletes healthier.

CONSIDERATIONS BEFORE OPTING FOR A SPORTS DRINK

PARENTS SHOULD CONSIDER a few critical points regarding sports drinks for teen athletes. Firstly, how long will the activity last? If an intense game or practice lasts over an hour, give your teen a sports drink for electrolyte replenishment and an energy boost. Next, consider the climate conditions; if it's hot and humid outside, you may want to ensure they hydrate well before their activity begins. Consider high school summer football practices and the extreme heat and humidity during this time of year, especially in the Midwest, South, and Southeast. Furthermore, swimmers are at particular risk of dehydration. Because in water, the bodies can't cool themselves with sweat that would generally cool an athlete when it evaporates. Also, the body is fooled into thinking it's not thirsty because they are literally in the water.

TEENS MUSTN'T OVERDO it when it comes to sports drinks - too much of a good thing can lead to health issues such as obesity or dental erosion from excessive sugar intake. Moderation is key. But which sports drink is best for teen athletes? Natural juice-based sports drinks, such as Mango Orange Fusion, are a good choice with natural fruit juices and electrolytes. Of course, plain water is still the best way to hydrate, so ensure your teen stays hydrated with their sports drink.

TEN PROS AND CONS OF SPORTS DRINKS

PROS OF SPORTS DRINKS:

- *Contain electrolytes* that are lost during physical activity or sweating
- *Replenishes energy stores* with carbohydrates
- *May contain vitamins and minerals*
- Helps to *balance fluid levels Improves performance*
- Can *replace lost electrolytes*
- *Improve hydration*
- *Boost energy*
- *Aids in recovery* after exercise

- *Enhances endurance*

Cons of Sports Drinks:

- Could be *high in calories*
- *High sugar content* can lead to weight gain if consumed regularly
- *Artificial colors, flavors, and sweeteners* could be present
- *Contain caffeine or other stimulants*
- May *irritate sensitive stomachs*
- May cause *tooth decay* from sugars
- Could *interact with medications*
- Could *increase the risk of developing Type 2 Diabetes*
- Generally, *more expensive than water*
- It could *increase the risk of kidney stones* if consumed too often

DIY Sports Drinks

These DIY sports drinks are much better for your teen athletes than the store-bought options because they contain no artificial flavoring or sweeteners – only natural ingredients that can help support their health. You can customize each recipe to fit their needs and taste preferences. These recipes will help keep your teen athlete well-hydrated and feeling great. (Water vs. Sports Drinks, n.d.)

_CITRUS COCONUT DRINK_ - Perfect for those who like a bit of sweetness with their hydration. Combine:

- coconut water
- freshly squeezed lime juice local honey*
- a pinch of Himalayan Sea salt

_GREEN SMOOTHIE_ -This green nutrient-packed superfood smoothie is perfect for an athlete who needs an extra boost. Combine:

- milk (your choice of type) spinach
- banana
- hemp seeds (if you have them)
- spirulina powder (if you have it)
- local honey*

_BERRY SPRITZER_ - This berry spritzer is just the ticket for athletes who want something light and bubbly. Combine:

- coconut water
- frozen mixed berries
- lime juice
- local honey*
- club soda

*CHIA FRESCA* - This chia fresca is ideal for those who need extra electrolytes. Combine:
   coconut water or filtered water
   chia seeds
   local honey*
   freshly squeezed lemon juice
   a pinch of sea salt

*HONEY HAS MANY HEALTH BENEfiTS. Its compounds help restore proper electrolyte balance and reduce inflammation. Additionally, if you can get local honey, it is said to help reduce allergy symptoms. Typically, local farmers' markets have local honey.

## PROTEIN DRINKS: BENEfiTS AND CONSIDERATIONS

ATHLETES of all ages need protein, but it's essential for teens. It helps them build and maintain strong muscles and provides the energy to power through practices and games. Protein can also help with recovery after strenuous workouts or competitions.

PROTEIN SHAKES CAN BE a great way for teen athletes to get the extra nutrients they need to perform at their peak. They are fast and convenient, easy to prepare, and packed with protein and other essential nutrients that will help support muscle growth and repair. Protein shakes are also great when they don't have time for a complete meal but still want to ensure they get the essential nutrition their bodies need.

## DOES PROTEIN MAKE TEEN ATHLETES STRONGER?

IF YOUR YOUNG athlete wants to bulk up, a diet with more protein may help. Protein helps build muscle and aids in recovery after exercise. That said, it's not just about the quantity of protein – quality matters too. Aim to get most of your proteins from lean sources like organic meat, then pair that protein with nutritious carbs such as quinoa, brown rice, oats, or sweet potatoes for the best results. If you want to give your sports star an extra edge on the field, ensure they get enough good-quality protein in their diet. It won't guarantee success, but it might give them that competitive edge.

### TIMING OF PROTEIN CONSUMPTION

IF YOUR TEEN wants to get the most out of their training sessions, they must focus on choosing high-quality proteins rich in essential amino acids and ensuring they eat them at the correct times throughout the day. Consuming 20-40g of complete protein sources 2-3 hours before and within 30 minutes after exercise is ideal for muscle growth and repair.

ADDITIONALLY, ensuring that your teen's pre-workout meal contains complex carbohydrates will help keep their energy levels up during exercise, while adding a moderate amount of healthy fats helps slow digestion so that the nutrients can release steadily into the bloodstream. By considering the importance of protein timing and the type and amount of protein consumed, you'll be helping your teen get the most out of their training sessions while providing the nutrients they need to stay healthy and active. Now that's something to be proud of. (Braddock, 2021)

## NATURAL SOURCES OF PROTEIN

- *Eggs* offer an excellent source of high-quality protein at an affordable cost. They contain all nine essential amino acids and are a great addition to any meal or snack. Hard-boiled eggs make for quick prep and easy transport if your teen needs something quickly and on the go.
- *Beans and Legumes* are also good sources of plant-based protein. They're packed with fiber, vitamins, and minerals too. Our son ate a bean and cheese burrito on a whole-wheat tortilla for breakfast almost every day of his entire high school career. The burrito and a protein drink provide him with long-lasting energy and nutrients needed for a teen scholar and athlete. Try throwing some black beans into a wrap for lunch or snack on edamame as an afternoon pick-me-up.
- *Nuts and Seeds* are another easy way to get protein – but don't forget the portion size. A handful goes a long way in helping meet daily protein goals. Add them to everything from oatmeal to yogurt and salads for a nutrient-packed punch. Our teen athletes had peanut butter and honey on whole-grain bread with chocolate organic whole milk almost daily on the way home from practice.
- *Organic, Grass-Fed Meats* provide complete proteins for your athlete. Meats like beef, chicken, turkey, lamb, and fish are excellent protein sources. Organic, Grass-Fed meats offer all the nutrients

without the chemicals or hormones commonly occurring in mass-produced meats. Cooking up some chicken on the weekend to have it available during the busy time of the week. The chicken can go into salads, pasta, wraps, and more!

## Types of Protein Powders Available

Protein powders are becoming increasingly popular among teen athletes looking to gain muscle and maintain a healthy weight. Protein is essential for building and maintaining muscle mass, so teens must get enough of this nutrient. But with so many types of protein powders on the market, knowing which type is best for teen athletes can be challenging. There are three main types of protein powder: whey, casein, and plant-based proteins.

- **_Whey Protein_** is derived from dairy products contains all nine essential amino acids the body needs digests quickly, making it ideal for post-workout recovery or as an extra nutrition boost in the morning.
- **_Casein Protein_** is another dairy-based powder slowly releases amino acids, making it useful for sustained energy throughout the day.
- **_Plant-Based_** proteins such as soy, pea, and hemp offer all nine essential amino but may also contain added vitamins and minerals like iron and omega-3s.

WHEY OR PLANT-BASED proteins usually work best when choosing the best protein powder for teen athletes. Whey is quickly digested and can help with muscle repair after an intense workout session, while plant-based proteins are a good source of fiber and other nutrients that can boost energy levels during workouts.

ULTIMATELY, the best protein powder for your teen athlete is entirely up to their preference. My son and I find some protein powders unpleasant in taste, and our daughter has found certain brands to give her an upset stomach. To ensure they have the most beneficial product, keep track of what protein powders they consume and how they feel and perform afterward. With this information, you can quickly determine which brand suits them best.

## DIY PROTEIN SHAKES

STORE-BOUGHT protein shakes can be expensive and loaded with sugar and artificial ingredients. One can easily make protein shakes at home. Control the ingredients in the shake—without any of the unhealthy stuff. Plus, homemade protein shakes are more affordable than those bought in stores and you can tailor the shake around what your teen athlete likes.

*CHOCOLATE PEANUT BUTTER HEAVEN*. Blend:

- 1 cup of cold milk of your choice
- 1 tablespoon of nut butter of your choice
- ½ scoop of chocolate whey powder

- ¼ teaspoon of cinnamon
- 1 banana

*TROPICAL GREEN PROTEIN SHAKE.* Give your teen an island vacation right at home with this smoothie. Blend:

- ¾ cup frozen mango cubes
- ½ frozen banana
- 2 tablespoons of chia seeds
- 1 scoop of vanilla protein powder
- 1 cup of cold milk of your choice

*PB&J Protein Shake.* If your teen still craves childhood nostalgia, this one's for them! Blend:

- ½ cup of frozen strawberries
- 1 tablespoon of peanut butter
- ¼ cup of oats 1 scoop of vanilla or chocolate whey protein powder
- 1 cup of cold milk of your choice

## EXCESS INTAKE OF PROTEIN

THERE ARE potential consequences of excess protein consumption of which to be aware. Eating an excessive amount can lead to dehydration, fatigue, nausea, kidney problems, and even liver damage. It's also possible for people with high-protein diets to become deficient in vital minerals like calcium or iron. A food log should help monitor protein intake and how athletes respond to certain foods- the types and quantities.

## Supplements: An In-Depth Guide

WITH HIGH ENERGY DEMANDS, teen athletes sometimes struggle to meet their nutrition needs through regular food intake alone. That's why dietary supplements can be valuable to a teen athlete's diet. With careful consideration of safety and efficacy, supplements might provide the extra boost they need without compromising nutrition.

SUPPLEMENTS LIKE PROTEIN POWDERS, creatine, amino acids, bars, pre-workout supplements, and more provide essential nutrients for optimal athletic performance. Not only do they help athletes achieve peak levels of fitness, but they can replace meals when time is tight or simply as an addition to their regular diet. (Dietary Supplements & Young Athletes: Unravelling Fact from Fiction, n.d.)

## Potential Dangers with Supplements

DIETARY SUPPLEMENTS for teen athletes can be a great way to support performance and optimize nutrition. Plenty of dietary supplement options exist if your teen athletes want an extra edge in the gym or on the track. These products can give them more energy, increase endurance, build muscle mass, and even aid post-workout recovery. But as with any supplement, it's critical to understand the potential risks.

THE FDA DOES NOT REGULATE dietary supplements like prescription and over-the-counter medications. This lack of oversight makes it difficult to know what's in them, how they'll interact with your athlete's biology, and any other medications they may be taking. Unregulated supplements can also potentially contain harmful contaminants like lead, arsenic, and mercury that can cause long-term health issues. When buying supplements look for USP, NSF, and other "seals of approval" from third-party verification.

TALKING to your teen about why taking unregulated dietary supplements isn't worth the risk is essential. Other athletes may share with them experiences using supplements that may not be appropriate for your teen athlete. One of the biggest concerns is anabolic steroid use, which some would consider a "supplement." Ensure your teen athlete understands that natural supplements aren't always safe and that there are better ways to get all the nutrients their body needs to stay healthy and perform their best.

## TECH TOOLS FOR NUTRITION MANAGEMENT

MOBILE NUTRITION TRACKING apps offer teenage athletes and their parents a convenient way to monitor dietary intake and achieve performance goals. By scanning barcodes or searching an app's database, these apps provide immediate access to the nutritional information of foods and beverages. Users can log meals and snacks, track macronutrients like protein and carbs, and receive alerts if they fall short of or exceed their targets. This data shows how nutritional choices impact health and athletic performance, empowering teen athletes to balance their diets effectively. For parents, nutrition apps offer peace of mind through insight into their teen's eating habits and an opportunity to guide to support proper growth and development. With busy schedules and limited time, these apps save effort and reduce guesswork around sports nutrition. Look for a list of apps in the "Resource Section."

FOOD DELIVERY SERVICES

FOOD DELIVERY SERVICES targeting athletes tailor to the specific dietary needs of individuals engaged in rigorous physical training. For teen athletes with demanding practice and game schedules, these specialized meal delivery services can be hugely convenient and helpful for meeting nutritional goals, especially considering the busy schedule everyone seems to have.

HOWEVER, the suitability of these services varies based on several factors. For athletes with specific dietary restrictions or allergies, many meal delivery services offer customizable menus and options for various dietary needs, such as paleo, vegan, and gluten-free. Teen athletes aiming to gain muscle may benefit from high-protein meal options, while those looking to maintain a leaner physique may prefer lower-carb or lower-calorie meals. Regarding budget, while some specialized delivery services may be more affordable than purchasing and preparing specialized ingredients and meals individually, others can be expensive, especially if ordering for a whole family.

PARENTS OF TEEN athletes need to evaluate their children's specific goals, family preferences, and budgets to determine if a specialized food delivery service is suitable. While convenient, these services are not a one-size-fits-all solution, and parents should gauge if using a delivery service would adequately meet their teen's nutritional needs relative to other options. If you've decided to try a service, look for flexible plans, reasonable pricing, and healthy, flavorful meals with options your teen will enjoy. Check our resources page for a list of meal supply options.

IN CONCLUSION, while protein shakes, sports drinks, and supplements seem like appealing options to help teen athletes meet their nutritional needs, they can be unnecessary, expensive, or even harmful. A balanced diet of whole foods with adequate calories and all the major nutrients is the healthiest and most effective way for teen athletes to fuel their activity. In the next chapter, we will explore dietary restrictions teen athletes may face, such as vegetarian or vegan diets, food allergies or intolerances, or disordered eating, and how to ensure proper nutrition within the context of these challenges. With guidance, support, and education about balanced and sustainable eating, teen athletes can learn positive habits to support their sports performance and overall growth and development.

# 9

## DIETARY AND EATING LIFESTYLE RESTRICTIONS

I s your teen athlete allergic to peanuts? Vegan by choice? Keeping kosher? Whatever your teenager's dietary needs and preferences, you need the knowledge and strategies to provide them with the optimal nutrition they need to stay healthy and strong. This chapter will help equip you with everything you need to know about how to properly fuel your young athletes, given dietary restrictions or lifestyle diets, so that they can perform their best.

BEING the parent of a teen athlete with allergies and dietary restrictions can be a difficult challenge. Years ago, while training a female athlete, I was very concerned about her vegetarian diet. Her mother and I would often discuss the challenges regarding meeting her nutritional needs while aligning with her vegetarian lifestyle. We both felt she wasn't getting the nutrition she needed as her energy levels struggled to stay up with her training demands. Additionally, her ability to grow and maintain her muscle mass was hindered by her diet, and she got sick often. All signs of her body not getting enough of the proper nutrients. Luckily, we devised a 28-day meal plan combining her nutritional needs and her vegetarian desire. Once we got her on the meal plan, ensuring she got the nutrients she needed, I saw changes in her body, attitude, and skin. Thank goodness! She was a perfect example of what happens without proper nutrition. Your child may be unable to perform at their best during practices or games, get sick more often, and their mental health can suffer with dietary restrictions; that's why it is essential to develop creative meal plans that meet the needs of your teen athlete's specific diet. By reading this chapter, you will better understand how to cater to your teen athlete's dietary needs. With these strategies, you can confidently provide nutritious meals for your child that meet their unique nutritional requirements while allowing them to enjoy the foods they love.

## DIET CONSIDERATIONS

PARENTS of teenage athletes have a unique challenge in providing their children with balanced nutrition and optimal athletic performance. The dietary needs of teen athletes can vary significantly from those with specific allergies, or IBS, to vegans or vegetarians. Parents must understand these considerations when planning meals for their children to ensure they receive the proper nutrients for peak performance.

WHEN IT COMES to allergen-free diets, there should be an emphasis on avoiding food sensitivities as much as possible while still meeting nutritional requirements. This plan means substituting any allergenic foods, like wheat, dairy, egg, etc., for alternatives that provide the same essential vitamins and minerals. Additionally, special precautions may need regarding cross-contamination during the food preparation process are a consideration. When our daughter was around four years old, we discovered she had an allergy to kiwi fruit. Her reaction was so severe her doctor prescribed an epipen in case she accidentally ingested kiwi fruit. Additionally, she wore a medic alert bracelet to alert any first responders of her allergy. My biggest concern wasn't that she would eat a kiwi but that she would eat a fruit salad that had been cross-contaminated with kiwi fruit.

FINALLY, those with IBS can benefit from a low-FODMAP diet which aims at reducing symptoms triggered by fermentable carbohydrates like garlic, onion, honey, and certain fruits and vegetables. Foods high in soluble fiber may also cause digestive upset, so it is essential to identify these triggers and plan meals accordingly.

PROVIDING teens with balanced nutrition and optimal performance requires parents to consider their dietary needs and constraints. Let us discuss every detail of creating a diet plan to help your teen excel in sports. With the proper care and attention, you can ensure your child receives everything they need to perform their best.

VEGETARIAN DIET

VEGETARIAN AND VEGAN diets are growing in popularity among teen athletes as well. A vegetarian diet is an eating pattern that excludes or limits animal products such as meat, poultry, fish, and seafood. Teen athletes may choose this lifestyle for ethical, health, environmental, or religious reasons. There are several different types of vegetarian diets depending on the level of food restriction. However, it is essential to recognize that these diets may require additional supplementation to maintain balanced nutrition. Vegetarians must ensure they get adequate protein, while vegans must be extra diligent about meeting their iron and B12 needs. Parents should consult a sports performance and nutrition counselor when planning meals for their vegetarian or vegan athletes to ensure they receive all the nutrients required for peak athletic performance.

ESSENTIAL AMINO ACIDS are the building blocks of proteins, and they're necessary because our body can't make them on its own. Our bodies must obtain them through diet. Incomplete proteins don't contain all nine essential amino acids, whereas complete proteins do. Therefore, complete proteins are more valuable for maintaining a healthy and balanced diet as they provide us with the full spectrum of nutrients, we need to stay healthy. Eating complete proteins has been linked to increased muscle mass, better growth, stronger immunity, lower risk of metabolic disorders, and improved bone health.

FOR VEGETARIAN TEENAGE ATHLETES, it is vital to include complete proteins in their diet. Vegetarian diets may require more planning and forethought to ensure they get the full range of essential amino acids. Plant sources such as nuts, legumes, quinoa, and green leafy vegetables can provide sufficient nutrition when eaten with other plant-based foods. Additionally, there are now many options for vegetarian protein powders that can supplement a balanced diet plan and help support peak performance for teenage athletes. By taking the time to understand the needs of their bodies correctly and eating a healthy variety of complete proteins, vegetarian teenagers will be able to maintain an active lifestyle with maximum energy and minimal fatigue.

## IMPORTANCE OF PROTEIN IN VEGETARIAN DIET

FOR VEGETARIANS, it is essential to understand how important protein is in their diet. Protein plays an integral role in the growth and development of various bodily functions, such as maintaining muscle mass, aiding digestion, helping with hormone regulation, and more. Unfortunately, some vegetarian diets cannot always fulfill the demand for proteins needed by the body without consideration of incomplete and complete proteins.

THEREFORE, vegetarians must take specific steps to ensure their diet provides enough protein. Ensuring adequate protein intake can be done in a variety of ways:

1. *Nuts and Legumes provide an excellent source of plant-based proteins, which can help meet daily requirements without resorting to meat or fish products.*
2. *Dairy Products such as milk and cheese can also help to increase protein intake. For those looking for an even more natural and plant-based approach, foods such as quinoa, hemp seeds, chia seeds, and spirulina all provide a good source of proteins.*
3. *Certain Vegetables in one's diet, such as broccoli or spinach, can also help to boost protein intake.*

IT IS important to remember that vegetarians should be mindful of the type and number of proteins they consume to ensure their body gets all the necessary nutrients. By planning meals carefully and considering various sources of proteins available to them, vegetarians can gain the bulk of their daily protein requirements. (Shereen Lehman, 2005)

## COMMON TYPES OF VEGETARIAN DIETS:

### LACTO-OVO-VEGETARIAN DIET:

THE LACTO-OVO-VEGETARIAN diet is becoming increasingly popular among teen athletes. This diet consists of plant foods and animal products derived from eggs and dairy but excludes all other animal products such as meat, poultry, fish, and seafood. It has many benefits that can help improve the performance of teenage athletes. Principals of the Lacto-Ovo-Vegetarian Diet:

- *Eggs* (ovo) are allowed. (*No meat, poultry, seafood, or fish*)
- *Most widely practiced form of vegetarianism.*
- *Packed with essential nutrients that can provide teens with the energy and strength needed to excel in their chosen sport.*
- *The diet usually contains a variety of plant proteins, such as legumes and grains, which are excellent sources of protein that are low in fat and fiber.*
- *Dairy products like yogurt, milk, and cheese are excellent sources of calcium, Vitamin D, and other essential vitamins.*

- *High in antioxidants that can help reduce inflammation.*
- *Can improve muscle recovery time after workouts and reduce the risk of injury due to overtraining.*
- *This diet may positively affect the digestive system, making it easier to absorb essential nutrients and lowering symptoms of gastrointestinal distress.*

THE LACTO-OVO-VEGETARIAN DIET helps promote a healthier lifestyle overall. It is low in saturated fats and high in fiber, which can help lower cholesterol levels and reduce the risk of diabetes, heart disease, and other chronic conditions. Additionally, because teens tend to consume more sugary drinks and processed foods than adults, a vegetarian diet can help them practice healthier eating habits that they can carry into adulthood. Additionally, the Lacto-Ovo-Vegetarian diet is an excellent option for teen athletes looking to improve their performance and health. Its combination of plant proteins, dairy, and antioxidants can give teens the energy, strength, and nutrients needed to achieve their athletic goals. If one addresses the nutritional limitations, this type of diet should be able to fuel your athlete adequately. Principals and Benefits of the Lacto-Ovo-Vegetarian Diet:

- *Eliminates all animal products except dairy.*
- *Can off er a wide range of vitamins, minerals, and fiber.*
- *Can be beneficial for those looking to lose weight. Since it eliminates processed and fatty foods.*
- *Vegetarian diets are often low in saturated fat and cholesterol, so they can help reduce the risk of heart disease and other health issues associated with consuming animal products.*

HOWEVER, the downside of following a Lacto-Vegetarian diet as an adolescent athlete is that this type of diet does not provide the necessary protein intake to support adequate muscle growth and strength needed for optimal athletic performance. While plant sources are available, such as legumes, nuts, and seeds, lack certain essential amino acids found in animal proteins. Teen athletes should incorporate plant-based proteins such as quinoa, and tempeh if they want to follow a vegetarian diet. Additionally, teens must supplement their diets with other protein sources, such as eggs, dairy products, or fortified non-dairy milk, to ensure they get the necessary nutrients to support athletic performance. Furthermore, with a vegetarian diet, teens often struggle to meet their daily requirement of calories and other essential vitamins and minerals for growth and development. And, like Lacto-Ovo-Vegetarians, these athletes are at risk of developing anemia. Those on a Lacto-Vegetarian diet should focus on getting enough protein and calcium from plant sources like those mentioned above. Additionally, they can look for supplemental sources of Vitamin B12, such as fortified cereals or nutritional yeast. Not only do these athletes tend to miss out on Vitamin B12, teen athletes who follow a Lacto-Ovo-Vegetarian diet may also risk missing out on some essential nutrients. Protein is one of the most important nutrients for athletes, and while some plant sources contain protein, it is often incomplete and may not provide enough to meet an athlete's needs. Additionally, vegetarians tend to have lower iron stores due to the lack of heme iron found in animal foods, which can lead to anemia or low red blood cells in the blood. Anemia can hinder oxygen accessibility from the bloodstream since red blood cells carry oxygen to the cells to create energy. Calcium and zinc are also essential minerals for athletes, but they are sometimes limited on a vegetarian diet if dairy products are not consumed or fortified foods are not included.

## Ovo-Vegetarian Diet:

AN OVO-VEGETARIAN DIET is a plant-based eating plan that includes eggs as the only animal protein. This diet emphasizes a variety of fruits, vegetables, whole grains, legumes, nuts, and seeds, providing a rich array of vitamins, minerals, and fiber. The inclusion of eggs offers a good source of essential nutrients such as protein, vitamin B12, and choline, which can sometimes be challenging to obtain from plant foods alone. An Ovo-Vegetarian diet supports overall health and can be beneficial for heart health, weight management, and reducing the risk of chronic diseases. Principals and Benefits of the Ovo-Vegetarian Diet:

- *Focuses on plant-based foods such as fruits, vegetables, legumes, grains, and nuts while also allowing for the consumption of eggs.*
- *This diet provides an excellent source of nutrition and energy that can help keep teenagers energized during their training and competitions.*
- *Low in saturated fat, cholesterol, refined sugars, and sodium yet still provides essential vitamins, minerals, and fiber - all of which are important for the physical development of teenagers as they continue to grow.*
- *Helps reduce the risk of chronic illnesses such as obesity, type 2 diabetes, and heart disease.*

THE DOWNSIDE of following an Ovo-Vegetarian diet for teen athletes is that getting the proper balance of proteins, carbohydrates, and fats needed for optimal performance takes effort and planning. Ovo-Vegetarian athletes may struggle with getting adequate protein in their diet but can meet these requirements by eating eggs, legumes, nuts, and soy products. As with other vegetarian diets, it is essential that they get a good amount of iron from leafy greens like spinach or collard greens and add fortified foods to provide Vitamin B12. Without animal sources of these macronutrients, teens may be able to rely on plant-based sources, which are less nutrient-dense or require more time to prepare. Additionally, some athletes may need help to consume enough calories from plant-based sources to support their high-energy demands. Lastly, without animal protein sources, teen athletes who follow an Ovo-Vegetarian diet may be able to supplement with vitamins and minerals such as iron and B12, which can be found in animal products but are scarce in plant-based foods. Following an Ovo-Vegetarian diet can be an excellent way for teen athletes to gain the health benefits of a vegetarian lifestyle. Still, pay to ensure they get all the nutrients needed for optimal performance.

PESCATARIAN DIET

A PESCATARIAN DIET is a type of eating plan that includes fish and seafood as the primary sources of protein. This diet often incorporates a variety of plant-based foods, including fruits, vegetables, whole grains, legumes, nuts, and seeds, making it rich in essential nutrients and fiber. This diet can offer a balanced approach to nutrition, combining the benefits of a vegetarian lifestyle with the added advantages of high-quality protein and healthy fats from seafood. Principals and Benefits of a Pescatarian Diet:

- *Fish only as a meat source*
- *Omega-3 fatty acids found in fish can help reduce inflammation*
- *Improve immune function*
- *Help increase cognitive function.*
- *Protein content of fish can help promote muscle growth and strength*
- *Low-calorie, nutrient- dense energy source for athletes.*
- *Can help to reduce an individual's risk of developing chronic health conditions such as high blood pressure, diabetes, and certain types of cancer.*
- *Can help to reduce cholesterol levels and improve overall cardiovascular health.*
- *Fish are excellent sources of vitamin D, calcium, iron, magnesium, and zinc—all essential nutrients for bone formation and muscle repair.*
- *Dietary sources of vitamin B12, which helps to keep the nervous system functioning correctly.*

FOLLOWING a Pescatarian Diet as a teen athlete can be difficult, especially if teammates and friends follow different diets. Consuming enough protein is vital for the body to stay healthy and nourished while engaging in strenuous physical activity. Fish and other seafood are excellent sources of lean protein but may be one of many options for meeting caloric requirements. Eating a variety of lean proteins, grains, and vegetables is essential for any athlete. Additionally, it can be challenging to find food options that fit within a pescatarian diet while attending sporting events or traveling out of town. Following this diet can lead to inadequate nutrient intake, hindering an athlete's performance, especially during travel.

ADDITIONALLY, I strongly warn against eating "farm-raised fish." These fish don't have the same nutritional value as fresh-caught fish and may also have harmful chemicals that we all try to avoid in our diets. Furthermore, farm-raised fish can harm the environment and wild fish populations. Lastly, even canned tuna is not without its risks. Tuna can have high levels of mercury and should not be consumed daily.

## FLEXITARIAN DIET:

A FLEXITARIAN DIET, also known as a semi-vegetarian diet, is a flexible eating plan that primarily focuses on plant-based foods while allowing for occasional consumption of meat and other animal products. This diet emphasizes fruits, vegetables, whole grains, legumes, nuts, and seeds, providing a rich source of essential nutrients and fiber. Flexitarians aim to consume meat in moderation, often choosing high-quality, ethically sourced options when they do. The flexibility of this diet makes it easier for athletes to adopt and maintain, as it does not require strict elimination of any food groups. By reducing meat intake and increasing plant-based foods, this diet can support weight management, improve heart health, and lower the risk of chronic diseases, while still accommodating individual prefer-ences and nutritional needs. Principals and Benefits of the Flexitarian Diet:

- *Improved digestion*
- *Allows for multiple protein sources*
- *Increased energy levels*
- *Better muscle growth*
- *Maintain a healthy weight while providing essential nutrients for optimal performance.*

- _Avoids processed food items containing added sugar or preservatives._

THE FLEXITARIAN DIET also encourages teenagers to be mindful of their food choices, as it emphasizes the importance of eating a balanced diet that includes a variety of foods. Eating more plant-based foods can reduce environmental impact and help teens become more aware of the sources of their food, as well as the potential consequences of their dietary choices.

BUT TEEN ATHLETES who follow a Flexitarian Diet may not get the nutrients needed for optimal performance. Such diets are usually low in both carbohydrates and essential fatty acids, which can lead to reduced energy levels and decreased muscle mass. Additionally, these diets often need more protein for muscle growth and repair, meaning that teen athletes may need help to reach their full potential. Therefore, teen athletes should consult a sports performance and nutrition counselor before beginning a Flexitarian diet to ensure they get the nutrients necessary for optimal performance. Flexitarians may find it easier to meet their nutritional requirements since they are not limited to one type of diet. However, they should still ensure that most of their ingredients come from plant-based sources to get enough fiber and other plant nutrients, like fruits and vegetables.

THE FLEXITARIAN DIET can be an excellent choice for teenage athletes that helps them stay healthy and perform at their best. It provides a well-rounded diet with essential nutrients, reduces the risk of developing chronic health problems, and encourages responsible food choices. With its numerous benefits, it's no wonder that the trend of Flexitarian eating is growing among athletes.

## VEGAN DIET:

A VEGAN DIET is a plant-based eating plan that excludes all animal products, including meat, dairy, eggs, and honey. Instead, it focuses on a diverse range of foods such as fruits, vegetables, whole grains, legumes, nuts, and seeds. This diet is rich in essential nutrients like fiber, vitamins, and minerals, while typically being lower in saturated fats and cholesterol. Vegans often emphasize whole, minimally processed foods to ensure they obtain sufficient protein, iron, calcium, and vitamin B12 from plant sources or supplements. A well-planned vegan diet can support overall health, aid in weight management, and reduce the risk of chronic diseases such as heart disease, diabetes, and certain cancers. Additionally, many people choose a vegan lifestyle for ethical reasons, including animal welfare and environmental sustainability. Principals and Benefits of a Vegan Diet:

- *Avoids all animal products, including dairy, eggs, meat, poultry, fish, and seafood.*
- *Full of various vitamins, minerals, and other essential nutrients.*
- *Plant-based proteins, like those found in beans and legumes, provide the body with all the amino acids it needs to build strong muscles.*
- *Complex carbohydrates such as whole grains give athletes long-lasting energy for their workouts.*

- *Plant-based foods are also packed with dietary fiber, which helps keep the digestive system healthy.*
- *Vegans also tend to have lower cholesterol levels than non-vegans. Lower cholesterol may help protect teen athletes from the risk of cardiovascular diseases.*
- *A plant-based diet also contains plenty of antioxidants that help fight inflammation and disease and vitamins and minerals that can improve immunity and prevent illness.*

OVERALL, the numerous benefits of a vegan diet make it an ideal choice for teen athletes who want to stay healthy, perform better in sports, and help protect the planet. However, one of the vegan athletes' most significant challenges is ensuring adequate intake of nutrients like vitamin B-12, calcium, iron, and omega-3 fatty acids. For example, vegan athletes can get vitamin B-12 from fortified foods (like breakfast cereals) or supplements. Dark green leafy vegetables contain calcium, as well as fortified foods. Additionally, plant sources high in iron (such as legumes and whole grains) should be included in the diet, along with fruits with plenty of Vitamin C to help maximize absorption. Lastly, vegan athletes should have walnuts and flax seeds daily to provide adequate omega-3 fatty acids.

WITH PROPER PLANNING and nutrition education, vegan athletes can perform at a high level, given the many advantages of a vegan diet. It's important to remember that balance is critical, and, taking steps toward maintaining optimal health (both physical and mental) should be a top priority. With the proper guidance, vegan athletes can enjoy all the benefits of plant-based eating.

THESE VARIOUS TYPES of vegetarianism have developed as some teen athletes look for ways to combine their philosophy on animal rights with the foods they are willing or able to eat. Teen athletes who practice a particular style of vegetarianism may benefit from specific health outcomes; however, it's essential to ensure an adequate variety and a balance of nutrients regardless of which type they choose. (Ajmera et al., 2018)

## TIPS FOR VEGAN AND VEGETARIAN ATHLETES TO MAINTAIN BALANCED NUTRITION.

### PLAN AHEAD

PLANNING IS critical to successful vegan and vegetarian nutrition for athletes. Planning meals and snacks and packing food for on-the-go situations can ensure that athletes get the nutrients they need without resorting to non-vegan or vegetarian options. Meal planning and prepping can be an effective way to plan nutrient-rich meals for the week, and athletes can keep vegetarian or vegan snacks on hand in case they're short on time. It may be beneficial for parents of teenage athletes to have family meal-planning sessions to brainstorm nutritious vegan and vegetarian options that will fit your teen's needs as an athlete. Being mindful of their nutrition is important no matter what kind of diet they follow. Ensuring your teen has access to healthy snacks and meals can help them get the energy and nutrition they need for their athletic performance. It can also help set them up for success in making good decisions as they grow older.

## Eat Plenty of Plant-Based Calcium

Calcium is an essential nutrient for athletes, vegan and vegetarian or not, as it helps build strong bones and teeth. It's a crucial nutrient for teen athletes whose bodies are still developing. Getting enough calcium can be tricky for vegans and vegetarians since dairy products are the primary source of this mineral in most diets—fortunately, plenty of plant-based calcium sources, such as dark green leafy vegetables, sesame seeds, and tahini. Encourage your teen athlete to include these in their diet to ensure they're getting enough calcium for optimal performance. Additionally, some vegan milk is fortified with extra calcium, so checking the nutrition label is good. With these tips, vegan and vegetarian athletes can ensure they're getting the calcium they need to fuel their performance.

## Don't Skimp on Healthy Fats

Parents of teenage vegetarian and vegan athletes should ensure their child gets enough healthy fats as part of their diet. Healthy fats are essential for growth, brain development, energy metabolism, hormone production, and other biological functions. Plant-based fat sources like avocados, nuts, seeds, olive oil, and nut butter provide important healthy fat sources. Additionally, including foods fortified with omega-3 fats like walnuts and soy milk can help meet the needs of an active teenage athlete. Healthy fats are essential for overall health and should be part of any vegan or vegetarian diet. Ensuring your teen gets enough healthy fat will ensure they get the nutrition they need to perform their best.

## GET ENOUGH VITAMIN B12

PARENTS OF TEEN athletes who follow a vegan or vegetarian diet should ensure their children get enough Vitamin B12. Vitamin B12 is found mainly in animal sources such as dairy, eggs, and fish. As such, vegans and vegetarians need to get adequate amounts of this essential vitamin through fortified foods, such as nutritional yeast, plant milk, and fortified breakfast cereals. Additionally, a vitamin B12 supplement is recommended for athletes who are vegan or vegetarian to avoid deficiencies in this critical nutrient.

BY TAKING these steps to ensure adequate Vitamin B12 intake, teen athletes following vegan and vegetarian diets can be confident they are getting the nutrition they need to support their active lifestyle.

REMIND your teen to speak to their doctor or a sports performance and nutrition counselor for advice on getting the right amount of Vitamin B12 and other essential nutrients. With some planning, vegan and vegetarian athletes of all ages can get the nutrition they need.

## KEEP "FAKE MEATS" TO A MINIMUM

PARENTS OF TEEN athletes following a vegetarian or vegan lifestyle should limit their child's consumption of "fake meats," such as veggie burgers and hot dogs. While these items can provide an easy meal solution, they are highly processed and laden with sodium and preservatives. Instead, parents should emphasize whole foods, such as beans, lentils, quinoa, and vegetables. These nutrient-dense options can be served in many forms – from salads to tacos to soups and stews – ensuring a balanced diet for the adolescent athlete. Additionally, look for plant- based protein sources that are more minimally processed, like tempeh or tofu. By serving these options, parents can help their teen athletes get the nutrition they need to power through their busy day.

## CHECK THE LABELS ON SPORTS NUTRITION PRODUCTS

FOR PARENTS of teen athletes who are vegan or vegetarian, it is essential to check the labels on sports nutrition products before purchasing. Many products contain animal-derived ingredients, so look for those labeled vegan-certified or plant-based ingredients. Also, ensure that any product you choose provides the right balance of vitamins and minerals needed to sustain an active lifestyle. The Academy of Nutrition and Dietetics suggests seeking fortified products such as breakfast cereals, nutritional yeast, meat substitutes, and energy bars for additional protein and nutrients. Fortified products will help ensure your teen gets the proper nutrition to stay healthy and perform at their best. However, I must admit I'm not a massive fan of fortified products since the "fortified" nutrients are not always bioavailable, meaning the body can't use the nutrients in the products. For more information on sports nutrition for vegan and vegetarian athletes, speak with a sports performance nutritionist. They can provide personalized advice and guidelines to help meet the unique dietary needs of your teen athlete. With proper planning and guidance, vegan and vegetarian athletes can still enjoy an active lifestyle while achieving their nutritional goals. (Rizzo, 2016)

## SUPPLEMENTS TO CONSIDER

IF YOUR TEEN athlete follows a vegan diet, it is important to ensure they get the proper nutrients. Calcium and Vitamin D are essential for vegan athletes as these nutrients primarily come from dairy products. To ensure your teen has enough of these two vitamins, consider having them supplement with calcium citrate and vitamin D2 or D3. Additionally, omega-3 fatty acids in fish oil can benefit heart health, so vegans may want to increase with algal oil. Finally, iron from plant sources like lentils and beans can be more challenging for the body to absorb than heme iron from animal sources; thus, vegan teens should also consider taking an iron supplement. With some intelligent supplementation choices, your teen can get the nutrients they need to perform at their best. (Vegan Diet: Foods, Benefits & More, n.d.)

## GLUTEN-FREE DIET/CELIAC DISEASE DIET:

THE GLUTEN-FREE/ Celiac disease diet is a particular way of eating that eliminates the consumption of foods containing gluten. Gluten is a protein found in wheat, barley, and rye. Teen athletes with Celiac disease need to follow a strict gluten-free diet to reduce their symptoms since even small amounts of gluten can cause damage to the intestinal lining. Following a gluten-free/Celiac disease diet can have several benefits, such as reducing inflammation, improving digestive health, and boosting energy levels.

WHEN FOLLOWING THIS DIET, it is crucial to focus on eating nutrient-dense foods that are naturally gluten-free. Nutrient-dense food includes fruits and vegetables, legumes, nuts and seeds, eggs, dairy products, fish and seafood, meat, poultry, rice, quinoa, flaxseed meal, and gluten-free grains such as buckwheat.

A GLUTEN-FREE DIET is important in fueling a young athlete for optimal performance. It can help improve energy levels, digestion, and overall well-being. But it can also be challenging to ensure the athlete gets all the necessary nutrients from such a restrictive diet. Carbohydrates are essential for young athletes because they provide a lot of energy for physical activity. Gluten-free complex carbohydrates like quinoa, buckwheat, and amaranth can be good energy sources for athletes on a gluten-free diet. Legumes such as chickpeas, lentils, and peas are also excellent protein sources.

FRUITS AND VEGETABLES should also be included in the diet, as they are a great source of vitamins and minerals. Gluten-free whole grains like corn, rice, and millet are also beneficial for providing energy. Luckily, producers are becoming more aware of the needs of celiac disease consumers and are offering a wider variety of options. COSTCO, for example, provides an excellent gluten-free flour blend.

EATING a balanced and varied diet is also vital for young athletes on a gluten-free diet to ensure they get all the necessary nutrients. Eating small meals throughout the day is recommended to help keep energy levels up and prevent overeating. (Julson et al., 2019)

## IRRITABLE BOWEL SYNDROME (IBS) DIET:

IRRITABLE BOWEL SYNDROME (IBS) is a chronic gastrointestinal disorder characterized by abdominal pain and altered bowel habit. Symptoms vary from person to person and can range from mild discomfort to severe pain. Common symptoms include abdominal cramping, bloating, flatulence, diarrhea, or constipation – sometimes alternating between the two. Other signs can consist of a feeling of incomplete evacuation and mucus in the stool.

TEEN ATHLETES SUFFERING from IBS may struggle to ensure the proper nutrition their body needs. Eating a balanced diet with adequate carbohydrates, proteins, and fats is essential for providing energy, building muscles, and repairing tissues during exercise. Foods rich in fiber, such as whole grains, legumes, and fruits, should also be included in your diet, as they help to improve digestion and can help reduce IBS symptoms. Additionally, foods with probiotics have been known to assist with digestion and can provide additional health benefits.

IT IS essential to keep track of how certain foods affect your symptoms. Certain high-fat or spicy foods, for example, may trigger IBS symptoms, so monitoring your intake and avoiding these triggers as much as possible is important. Also, avoid foods high in sugar or artificial sweeteners, as these can cause bloating and other digestive issues. Also, drink plenty of water daily to stay hydrated, which will help keep digestion regular and reduce symptoms.

FINALLY, when devising an athletic diet for athletes with IBS, paying attention to food allergies or sensitivities that may exacerbate the condition is essential. Eating a balanced diet without triggering foods can help teens manage their IBS symptoms while still being able to perform at their peak. With the proper diet, teens with IBS can reach their athletic goals while keeping up with their condition. (The Low FODMAP Diet: A Benefit for Athletes?, n.d.)

IN CONCLUSION, dietary restriction in teenage athletes is an important topic that parents should be aware of. It's not unusual for teen athletes to have specific meal requirements and/or restrictions due to their strenuous activity levels and unique needs. As parents, it is essential to ensure the nutrition of your teen athlete by providing nutritionally dense meals with appropriate macronutrients for energy, strength, and recovery. Furthermore, communication between parents, coaches, and athletes is key when navigating dietary concerns or needs and understanding the importance of fueling the body correctly for optimal performance. With a balanced diet approach, adequate hydration, and restful sleep cycles, you can help your teen maximize their athletic potential while maintaining good health.

# 10

## BLOOD SUGAR, HYDRATION, & SLEEP

Blood sugar levels are essential to overall health, especially for teen athletes. Blood sugar is a form of energy produced when food is broken down in the body and used to fuel muscle activity. Appropriately managing blood sugar helps ensure teens have enough energy to perform at their best during physical events or activities. When glucose (sugar) levels are low, it can cause fatigue, which affects performance and focus. Similarly, if glucose levels become too high due to not eating correctly before or during exercise, this can lead to sudden exhaustion or fainting. Thus, ensuring proper management of blood sugar levels in teenage athletes is key for optimal performance. Understanding the importance of blood sugar and how it impacts teen athletes is critical to maintaining youthful energy and physical activity. With proper nutrition, teens can stay energized and perform their best.

## Role Blood Sugar Levels & Mental Health

Teenage athletes must keep their blood sugar levels within a safe range. The best way to accomplish this is through proper nutrition: fueling nutrient-rich foods such as complex carbohydrates like whole grains, fruits, and vegetables; healthy proteins like lean meats or beans; and healthy fats such as nuts or avocado. Eating small meals regularly throughout the day can also help maintain steady energy levels without causing an extreme spike or drop in blood sugar levels. Hypoglycemia, or low blood sugar, can be dangerous for active teen athletes who require constant energy to fuel their physical activity. When blood sugar falls too low, it can lead to fainting spells and other serious health complications.

### Symptoms of Low Blood Sugar or Hypoglycemia:

1. _Fatigue_
2. _Irritability_
3. _Difficulty concentrating_
4. _Confusion_
5. _Anxiety_
6. _Depression_
7. _Feeling Shaky_
8. _Feeling weak_
9. _Rapid heartbeat_
10. _Sweating heavily_
11. _Blurred vision_

IF YOUR ATHLETE displays any of these symptoms during physical activity, it's best to stop all movement immediately and contact your healthcare provider for further guidance. It's also a good idea to have your athlete consume some form of sugar or carbohydrate to help restore their blood sugar levels.

## STRATEGIES FOR MAINTAINING BLOOD SUGAR LEVELS

*HEALTHY SNACKING*. Parents of teen athletes, we know that sports and healthy eating go hand in hand. As your teens commit to their sport, ensure they also pay attention to keeping up their energy levels with healthy snacking. Snacks can provide essential nutrients, increase alertness and help keep blood sugar levels steady throughout the day—all things an active teen needs. By snacking on nutritious foods such as fruits, vegetables, nuts, and seeds, your teen can fuel their body with vitamins and minerals while avoiding unhealthy sugars. Healthy snacks will also help regulate blood sugar levels—which is essential for peak athletic performance.

*PROPER NUTRITION.* To ensure proper nutrition before and after exercise, parents should encourage their teens to focus on carbohydrates that are low glycemic index (GI) foods. Examples include whole grains like oats, barley, and quinoa; vegetables like sweet potatoes, squash, and carrots; legumes like chickpeas and lentils; nuts; seeds; and dairy products. These are sources of slow-burning energy that will provide sustained fuel for activity — especially when combined with protein — and help keep blood sugar levels balanced.

*TIMING OF MEALS*. To prevent low blood sugar during activity, teens should have carbohydrates (such as fruit or whole grain toast) around 1-2 hours before exercise and a balanced meal within 2 hours after a workout. (Diabetes Diet, Eating, & Physical Activity, 2023)

*ADEQUATE CARBOHYDRATE CONSUMPTION*. First, ensuring that your teen gets adequate carbohydrates before participating in sports is important. Carbohydrates provide quick energy, which is essential for athletes during physical exertion - this will help prevent any drops in blood sugar during activity. Additionally, it's important to pack snacks and drinks that can help boost the athlete's sugar levels throughout the day - such as fruit juice, granola bars, and other carbohydrate-rich foods.

FINALLY, it's a good idea to educate your teen about the signs of hypoglycemia so they know when to seek medical attention. Symptoms include dizziness, weakness, trembling, faintness, or confusion - all of which should be taken seriously by athletes experiencing them. With careful planning and monitoring as a parent, you can help ensure your teen stays healthy and safe while engaging in their favorite sports activities.

WITH APPROPRIATE EDUCATION, support, and encouragement from parents, coaches, doctors, and other adults involved in teenage athletics, we can ensure better physical and mental health outcomes for our young athletes. By providing adequate hydration and steady blood sugar levels in teen athletes, we can create an environment that fosters our youth's physical and mental well-being. In conclusion, understanding and adhering to proper hydration and healthy eating habits is essential for teenage athletes' physical and psychological well-being.

## HYDRATION

HYDRATION IS integral to any teen athlete's success on the field or court. As such, teen athletes must be aware of the importance of proper hydration and take steps to ensure they remain adequately hydrated at all times. This chapter will discuss the benefits of hydration for teenage athletes and explain why it is so essential when striving for athletic excellence. By emphasizing how vital proper hydration is to success in sports, we hope to encourage teen athletes everywhere to stay mindful of their water consumption habits both on and off the field.

HYDRATION IS vital to staying healthy and maintaining a proper body balance. The science behind it is pretty simple: when we drink liquids, our bodies take the materials from those liquids (such as electrolytes) and use them to help cells regulate their functions, along with helping to transport oxygen throughout the body. Not only does hydration provide essential nutrients for the body, but it also helps flush out toxins and waste products that accumulate over time. Staying hydrated is essential so our cells can continue working optimally and keep us energized and alert. In addition, being properly hydrated helps improve blood circulation, reduce fatigue, and decrease muscle cramps or soreness after workouts.

THE HUMAN BODY is mostly water. Water aids digestion, transports nutrients, regulates temperature, and lubricates joints. It helps the body maintain its temperature and function correctly while exerting energy during physical activities. Proper hydration also aids in regulating blood pressure, removing toxins, and metabolizing nutrients for increased energy. Furthermore, it reduces fatigue and can help athletes prevent muscle cramps, strains, heat exhaustion, or heat stroke. When athletes aren't adequately hydrated, their bodies can't perform at the highest levels, and they become more susceptible to injury due to fatigue and dehydration. Being properly hydrated also helps maintain mental clarity on the field so that the athletes can stay focused and make better decisions when playing their respective sports. Proper hydration also keeps muscles nourished and healthy for maximum performance during physical activity and recovery afterward.

To ensure proper hydration, teens should drink plenty of water before physical activity begins, during breaks, or when exercising intensely. Rehydrating with homemade sports drinks containing electrolytes is a great way to replace minerals lost through sweat during extended workouts. By maintaining proper hydration levels, teens can maximize their athletic performance and avoid any health risks associated with dehydration. Dehydration can lead to fatigue, decreased performance, increased risk of injuries, and other complications. Therefore, teens must stay adequately hydrated before, during, and after strenuous activities or sports practices.

PROPER HYDRATION:

- **_Before_** training and competition, teen athletes should aim to drink at least 16 ounces (2 cups) of water two hours before any physical activity starts to prepare their bodies for the exertion ahead.

- *During* activities lasting longer than one hour, athletes should drink about 4-8 ounces (1/2 to 1 cup) of water every 15-20 minutes. Frequent hydration helps replace the fluids lost through sweat and keeps the body from becoming dehydrated. *Nearly 10,000 high school athletes suffer some heat-related illness annually that prohibits them from participating for one or more days after the event.*

- *After* training and competition, rehydration is as essential as pre-activity hydration; drinking fluid during physical activity will help replenish liquid sweat loss. However, it should not be limited to only immediately after the training has ended. Within two hours of an intense workout, teens should consume at least 16 ounces (2 cups) of water with electrolytes or natural juices like coconut water to remain hydrated.

- *Additionally*, ensure your teen has access to sodium-rich food, such as popcorn or pretzels, to help keep their electrolyte balance in check.

- *Don't Overload with Fluids*: While drinking water during exercise is important, drinking too much is possible.

## HYDRATION VS PHYSICAL & MENTAL HEALTH IN ATHLETES

HYDRATION PLAYS A VITAL ROLE IN TEENAGERS' physical health and well-being, particularly those involved in athletic activities. Proper hydration helps reduce fatigue, improves performance, regulates body temperature, and aids digestion. Athletes may experience dizziness, nausea, and decreased coordination without adequate hydration, which can significantly impact their performance. Furthermore, even slight dehydration can negatively affect an athlete's mood.

TO AID in proper hydration is to ensure that teens consume adequate electrolytes such as sodium and potassium. These minerals help regulate fluid balance within the body, promoting optimal hydration levels during physical activity. Some familiar sources of electrolytes include sports drinks, coconut water, and even certain fruits and vegetables, such as bananas and spinach.

### SYMPTOMS OF DEHYDRATION

DEHYDRATION CAN CAUSE a myriad of physical symptoms. When the body loses more fluids than it takes in, the blood volume decreases, and the heart must work harder. Parents of teen athletes must understand the signs and symptoms of dehydration to ensure their child is playing safely and competitively.

DEHYDRATION SYMPTOMS INCLUDE:

1. *Fatigue*
2. *Dizziness*
3. *Decreased coordination due to reduced oxygen delivery to muscles.*
4. *Muscle cramping increases exponentially as dehydration increases.*
5. *Headaches*
6. *Decreased performance ability*
7. *Irritability*
8. *Dry mouth*
9. *Thirst*

THE LOSS of electrolytes due to dehydration can increase susceptibility to muscle strain and injury from activities involving intense physical exertion. Therefore, proper hydration is an essential factor for athletes and exercisers alike. It is critical to stay properly hydrated before, during, and after exercise or activity to reduce the risk of suffering from any adverse effects caused by dehydration.

IF YOUR TEEN displays any of these signs during sports activity or practice, it's vital to stop the physical activity immediately and rehydrate. While they may feel disappointed in taking a break from their sport for safety reasons, it's always better to address dehydration sooner rather than later.

COMBAT DEHYDRATION by monitoring sweat rate and urine. Athletes should track how much fluid they lose via sweat to adjust their intake accordingly. The best way to do this is by weighing yourself before and after exercise, then subtracting the final weight from the initial weight to determine your sweat rate. A 2% change in body weight after an acute exercise can indicate dehydration. Especially true during hot times of the year when sweat and fluid losses are higher than normal. Keeping track of body weight before and after exercising can help maintain adequate hydration throughout the activity.

ADDITIONALLY, urinary track infections can be brought on by dehydration! So encourage your athlete, especially female athletes to keep their hydration levels up to combat this risk. Having a UTI is not fun and will sideline your athlete for days potentially!

ANOTHER WAY TO know how much fluid each athlete needs is by monitoring urine color and output. A darker yellowish hue indicates dehydration, while clear or very light-colored urine suggests that the person is adequately hydrated. Also, low levels of urine output can indicate dehydration. If your teen is serious about their sport, consider investing in a quality water bottle that's easily accessible and encourages frequent hydration breaks. Plastic bottles with water in them have dangerous chemicals that can leach into the water when exposed to heat-like on the sidelines during a hot day.

## OVER HYDRATION

PARENTS OF TEEN athletes may think that ensuring their child drinks enough fluids during their sports practices and games is always beneficial; however, over hydration can be just as dangerous. As a parent of a teenage athlete, it is vital to be aware of the risks associated with over hydration. Too much water can lead to *hyponatremia*, or an electrolyte imbalance in the body, caused by drinking excessive amounts of fluids without consuming enough sodium.

### SYMPTOMS OF OVER-HYDRATION INCLUDE:

1. *Nausea*
2. *Vomiting*
3. *Confusion*
4. *Fatigue*

THESE MORE SEVERE complications can lead to seizures and even death if left untreated. By following these tips, parents can help their teen athletes stay healthy and safe while still enjoying the benefits of physical activity. It's important to remember that safety should always come first in sports. With knowledge and preventative measures, you can ensure your teen's health and well-being for years.

## SLEEP-THE COMPETITIVE EDGE

SLEEP IS essential for teen athletes, just like a battery is essential for electronic devices. A battery provides the energy electronics need to operate and perform well. Lack of sleep, like a dead battery, can cause serious health issues. Therefore, teen athletes must get enough restful sleep at night to ensure optimal daily performance. Without enough sleep, it's difficult for teens to stay focused and energized during practices, games, and school. Quality, restful sleep is key for teenage athletes to reach their full potential in sports both physically and mentally and reach their performance goals. With it, they will have the energy they need to compete at a high level.

## THE IMPORTANCE OF SLEEP

ONE CANNOT OVERSTATE the importance of sleep. Getting enough sleep recharges the body for a new day and also aids in maintaining good physical and mental health. Our bodies are programmed to have regular sleep cycles, and disruptions in these can lead to severe consequences. Sleep is a naturally recurring state of mind and body characterized by altered consciousness, relatively inhibited sensory activity, reduced muscle activity, and inhibition of nearly all voluntary muscles during rapid eye movement (REM) sleep. It is a state of decreased responsiveness to external stimuli in which conscious awareness is entirely or partially lost. During this period, the brain processes information from recent events while consolidating memories and forming new ones. Various physiological processes during sleep help maintain physical health and affect mental well-being. Sleep helps restore energy levels due to its role in balancing hormones such as growth hormone, orexin A/hypocretin 1, serotonin, cortisol, and melatonin. It also helps regulate body temperature, heart rate, blood pressure, and breathing. Sleep is also essential for proper cognitive function; it helps improve concentration, alertness, problem-solving skills, creativity, and overall well-being. Studies suggest that even a small amount of regular sleep deprivation can lead to impaired judgment and emotional instability. ("Why Is Sleep so Important?" 2014)

BENEFITS OF SLEEP

SLEEP IS essential for our mental and physical health. Not only does it help us feel well-rested, but it also helps us stay alert and focused during the day. Research has shown that those who get enough sleep are likelier to have better overall health than those who don't. Getting adequate restful sleep helps keep our immune system strong, allowing us to fight off illnesses more effectively and recover quickly from any ailments we encounter. It also reduces inflammation that can aggravate or cause chronic diseases such as arthritis or diabetes. In addition, regular deep sleep helps reduce stress levels, improving mood and contributing to a healthier lifestyle overall.

SLEEP ALSO PLAYS a key role in maintaining a healthy weight. Studies have shown that sleep-deprived people eat more due to increased hunger hormones in the body. On the other hand, those who get enough restful sleep often have better control over their cravings and thus tend to make healthier choices regarding their diet.

GETTING enough quality sleep is also crucial for our cognitive performance. People who don't get sufficient restful sleep can struggle with memory recall and are less able to concentrate on tasks or learn new information quickly. Additionally, poor sleep can lead to slower reaction times and an inability to think clearly or complete simple tasks as efficiently as normal. (Day Writing Journals, 2019)

## IMPORTANCE OF SLEEP IN TEEN ATHLETES

SLEEP IS an essential part of life and even more so for teen athletes. Sleep helps to fuel their bodies with energy, repair any muscle damage from workouts, and improve their reaction time in sports. Truly, our bodies get stronger when we sleep. Studies have shown that a lack of sleep can lead to decreased athletic performance due to fatigue and reduced concentration. The National Sleep Foundation recommends at least 8-10 hours of sleep per night for teens and young adults. One can adjust the amount depending on individual physical activity levels and other factors such as age or health status. Teen athletes participating in high-intensity activities may need extra rest than those participating in low-intensity activities. Sleeping enough can be difficult for busy athletes juggling practice, schoolwork, and social activities simultaneously. But they need to prioritize their schedule to make time for adequate rest. Creating a consistent bedtime routine can help them get the required sleep each night.

OUR DAUGHTER WAS AN ELITE-LEVEL ATHLETE, often sleeping 8-10 hours nightly and taking 2-3 hours naps during the weekend and summer. All that physical activity required her to be well-rested; keeping her room dark and cool plus she wore earplugs to filter out any noise so she could get undisturbed sleep which is essential for her success. Eating well and getting quality sleep was equally crucial in meeting her training demands-both physically and mentally.

SLEEP DEPRIVATION in teen athletes is a serious issue that can have serious repercussions. Many teen athletes may need more than the recommended amount of sleep due to their busy schedules and the demands of their sports. The lack of sleep can lead to several signs and symptoms that may be mild at first but can worsen with time if the problem persists.

SIGNS AND SYMPTOMS OF SLEEP DEPRIVATION:

- *Decreased Energy Levels.* Teen athletes may struggle to perform optimally both during practice and competitions due to a lack of energy resulting from insufficient sleep. The body needs adequate sleep to restore and rebuild muscle tissues, allowing an athlete to feel energized for their sports activities. When the body doesn't get enough sleep, it does not have the time or resources to recover adequately, leading to feelings of fatigue from drinking coffee or eating sugary snacks. Drinking caffeine and eating nutrition-less food can be especially dangerous if athletes push their bodies without proper rest, leading to injury or burnout. Therefore, teen athletes need to ensure they get enough sleep each night to maximize their physical performance and stay healthy.

- *Difficulty Concentrating*. Teen athletes may struggle to pay attention or focus on tasks related to their sport due to inadequate restorative sleep. Sleep deprivation can hurt the ability of teen athletes to concentrate. Without adequate sleep, it becomes more difficult for teens to focus and remember information. As a result, their academic performance can suffer, as well as their athletic performance. Teen athletes not getting enough sleep report frequent foggy thinking or difficulty paying attention in class or during practices. Over time, their classroom and field performance may suffer if chronic sleep deprivation occurs. Teen athletes need to prioritize sleep so they can perform at their best both academically and athletically.

- *Memory Problems*. Sleep deprivation can cause difficulty remembering skills or techniques learned during practices or games. Teens who are new drivers and sleep-deprived can be a lethal combination. Lack of rest is known to impair judgment, reaction time, visual perception, memory, cognitive functions, and general alertness — all essential skills for athletes.

- *Poor Decision-Making*. Sleep deprivation can impair judgment, leading to increased risks for injury. When the body and mind are not well rested, it can lead to difficulty focusing and making decisions. As a result, athletes may struggle with making game-time decisions or even rush into decisions without fully considering their consequences. Poor decision-making is why athletic teens must prioritize quality sleep and be aware of signs that may indicate a lack of rest. Proper sleep can help these athletes make better decisions on the court or field, ultimately improving their performance and helping them reach their goals.

- **_Mood Swings and Irritability_**. Teen athletes may become easily frustrated and overwhelmed due to lack of sleep. Lack of sleep can cause teenagers to be more emotionally volatile, making them feel more easily irritated or upset than usual. They may also feel overwhelmed or unable to concentrate on tasks when they have not been getting enough rest. Teen athletes should pay close attention to their moods so that they can monitor any changes which may be related to their sleep habits. Experiencing moodiness can help athletes identify when to adjust to get the required rest each day. As a parent, you may need to quietly observe their moodiness instead of confronting your child about it. Confrontation, when they are already moody, is a recipe for disaster. Instead, try adjusting everyone's schedule to get more sleep and gently remind your athlete of the value of quality sleep.

- **_Higher Risk of Injuries_**. When tired, teen athletes are more likely to make mistakes resulting in preventable injuries. Lack of sleep can affect physical and cognitive performance. When the body is exhausted, reaction time slows, coordination decreases, and situational awareness diminishes. As a result, teen athletes may be more prone to accidents or fall short of their athleticism.

- **_Depression and Anxiety_**. Lack of sleep can also lead to mental health issues such as depression and anxiety. Studies show that those who don't get enough sleep are significantly more likely to suffer from depression and anxiety than their well-rested peers. Depression and anxiety can be very detrimental to an athlete's performance, making it difficult to focus or even enjoy the sport they used to love. Teen athletes must prioritize getting enough sleep to stay healthy and perform their best during games and practices.

- *Increased Stress Levels*. Lack of sleep can take its toll physiologically and psychologically. Our bodies use sleep to help recover from physically and emotionally stressful lives. Teen athletes are especially prone to elevated levels of adrenaline and cortisol due to the physical and mental demands associated with their sport. Adrenaline is a hormone released by the body in response to stress, excitement, or fear. This hormone helps teen athletes perform better during competition by boosting their energy, heart rate, and focus. Cortisol, on the other hand, is a hormone that helps their bodies recover from this "adrenaline surge." While it is beneficial in smaller doses, too much cortisol can lead to fatigue and impaired sleep quality.
- *Weakened Immune System*. Teen athletes are at an increased risk of developing a weakened immune system due to lack of sleep. Studies have shown that adolescents who get fewer than 8 hours of sleep per night are more susceptible to illness and infection, as their bodies cannot produce enough white blood cells for proper immune functioning. Lack of sleep also decreases the effectiveness of vaccinations, meaning protection from certain illnesses may be inadequate. In addition, research has found that even one poor night's sleep can significantly affect the body's natural defense mechanisms. One study found that after just one night with only 6 hours of sleep, participants had higher levels of cytokines,

which are proteins associated with inflammation and sickness. Teen athletes must prioritize adequate sleep to maintain a robust immune system for optimum performance and health.

* ***Poor Hormone Regulation.*** A lack of restorative sleep disrupts hormones like ghrelin which regulates hunger, and leptin, which controls energy balance.

ATHLETES ARE MORE prone to decreased performance and weight gain without proper rest. Adequate rest helps regulate hormones such as cortisol and leptin, controlling appetite and hunger.

IF YOU FEEL your athlete is struggling to communicate with their coach regarding their level of fatigue, you may need to step in and communicate directly with their coach. Since fatigue affects their academic performance, driving, and mental health, you must proactively correct the issue. I can tell you I've sent messages to my children's coaches and let them know they were exhausted and wouldn't be at practice so they could sleep in, nap, or rest. As a parent, my job is to protect their well-being and not let life run them ragged.

I WOULD ALSO LIKE to stress that sleep deprivation can be compared to "being under the influence." Reaction times are slowed, decision making is poor, concentration is lacking when one is sleep deprived. Please consider this before you let your teen behind the wheel of a car! If they are showing any of the symptoms listed above the risk of accidents greatly increases!

SETTING healthy boundaries and having conversations about the importance of rest and recovery can help teens understand why getting enough sleep is essential for their physical and mental health. Additionally, assisting teens in creating schedules that prioritize sleep may also be beneficial in ensuring they receive the necessary rest. By taking these steps, we can help teen athletes stay healthy and perform at their best - both on and off the field. By following these tips, teen athletes should be able to reduce their stress levels while maintaining performance in both school and sports. With adequate sleep, nutritious meals, and relaxation activities throughout the week, teen athletes will have the energy and focus necessary to succeed. (Grandner et al., 2021)

## STRATEGIES FOR GETTING REST AND SLEEP FOR TEEN ATHLETES

AS I MENTIONED our daughter was an elite-level athlete. She knew the importance of getting a good nights or days' rest, so she used earplugs to ensure that any noises around her wouldn't interfere with her sleep. She knew that using earplugs to minimize noise would improve her sleep, which could give her an added boost to her performance, mood, and immune function. Studies have shown that sleeping in absolute silence can help improve alertness and focus during physical activity, making it easier to concentrate and perform at the highest level.

SLEEP GIVES the body time to recover from strenuous activities and rebuild muscles, strengthens the immune system, and improves mental clarity. Teen athletes should aim for 8-10 hours of sleep per night to reap its many benefits and stay healthy for sports competitions. With intense practice sessions, competition events, and homework often piling up late into the night, it can be challenging to prioritize sleep over other activities. Teen athletes need to be aware of the consequences that sleep deprivation could have on their cognitive function and take steps to ensure they are getting enough rest. Achieving adequate rest will improve athletes' performance and help them stay focused and alert throughout the day. For the teen athlete, sleep is as important as practice and diet when optimizing performance. A consistent bedtime routine helps teens get the rest they need to stay healthy and perform their best on the field or court. Establishing a regular bedtime and limiting screen time before bed can help teens fall asleep faster and get enough sleep each night. Additionally, ensuring your teen's bedroom is dark, quiet, and comfortable encourages good sleeping habits that will pay off in athletic performance.

### Tips for Getting a Good Night's Sleep:

1. *Dark Room*-The teen athlete's room should be dark to ensure a good night's sleep. Darker rooms are more conducive to restful sleep, as the body perceives this environment as closer to natural nighttime outdoors. Blackout curtains or blinds can help reduce light pollution from outside sources, such as streetlights or car headlights, while helping keep the room cool during summer. Reducing ambient light levels will also help improve melatonin production and promote deeper, longer-lasting sleep for athletes needing extra rest to perform at their peak during physical activity.

2. *Quiet*- The teen athlete's room should be as quiet as possible for a good night's sleep. Ideally, noise in the bedroom should be kept to a minimum so that the teenager can rest and recover well from their daily activities. To minimize sound, consider using thick curtains or blinds to reduce outside sound distractions. It also helps to invest in acoustic wall treatments or soundproofing materials and solutions. Additionally, installing an air purifier can help filter out any sounds coming from other rooms in the house, improving overall quietness for better sleep quality. With these simple steps, the teen athlete can get the rest they need to perform at their best.

3. *Comfortable*- The teen athlete room should be comfortable for a good night's sleep. Selecting the right furniture and materials that will help create a cozy environment is crucial. A mattress with good support, such as memory foam, is recommended for athletes as they require more cushioning due to their active lifestyles. Choose pillows wisely, as side sleeping can provide additional comfort and reduce neck pain. Soft bedding in neutral colors like white or grey can add warmth and style to the room. Lastly, blackout curtains are essential for blocking out light so teens can get a full restful night of sleep. With these simple steps, the teen athlete room can become an oasis of comfort and relaxation where sports stars can maximize their performance.

4. *Calm Atmosphere*- Minimal distractions can help athletes relax and recharge before an upcoming game or competition. Calming scents such as eucalyptus, lavender, or vanilla can also help promote relaxation and restfulness. Music can also

create a peaceful environment, allowing teens to drift off into a deep sleep. Having a clear and organized bedroom also helps promote relaxation during sleep which is essential for recovery from strenuous physical activity and mentally preparing for future challenges in sports.

CREATE DESIGNATED areas for studying and relaxing away from electronics. And add these steps in:

- *Avoid Screen Time 1 Hour before Bed*-Avoid computer and phone screens in the bedroom so that athletes can escape the hustle and bustle of everyday life while preparing for their next event. Studies show reading a physical book can help relax the body and mind for a good night's sleep.

- *Remove Electronic Devices from the Bedroom*- Removing electronic devices from the bedroom can help teen athletes sleep better. Without access to devices like phones, computers, TVs, or video games in the bedroom, teens can reduce temptations that would otherwise keep them up at night or interfere with studying and restful sleep. In addition, by avoiding late-night use of electronics, teenage athletes will be less likely to suffer from a lack of focus due to fatigue caused by too much screen time.

- *Establish a Bedtime Routine* - Create a routine that includes regular sleep times, screen cut-off times, possibly an Epson salt bath, and reading a book to help the body and mind relax before bed.

- *Engage in Relaxation Techniques* - Relaxation techniques are essential for developing successful athletes. These techniques can help them improve their performance and reduce stress levels before or

after an event. Relaxation exercises such as deep
breathing, progressive muscle relaxation, guided
imagery, and yoga can all be beneficial in helping
teens manage the physical and mental demands of
sports. Deep breathing allows teens to regulate their
heart rate, while progressive muscle relaxation helps
teens relax their muscles from head to toe. Guided
imagery will enable teens to envision success by
picturing themselves performing at a high
level.These relaxation techniques help teen athletes
focus on the task while maintaining a healthy
balance between sports and other aspects of life.
There are many apps with guided meditation and
relaxation if your teen struggles with relaxing. Of
course, that combats the "no technology" rule, but
you and your teen will need to work that out.

- *Avoid Caffeine and Other Stimulants* - Teen athletes
should avoid using caffeine and other stimulants to
enhance their performance. These substances can
cause dehydration, irritability, increased heart rate,
gastrointestinal distress, anxiety, and difficulty
sleeping. They may also affect the body's natural
ability to perform long-term physical activities such
as running or playing sports. Additionally, excess
use of these stimulants can lead to higher levels of
stress hormones in the body which can negatively
affect athletic performance. Therefore, teen athletes
should strive for a balanced diet and healthy
lifestyle that does not rely on artificial stimulants for
improved performance. Similarly, drinking plenty of
water throughout the day will keep athletes
hydrated, reducing fatigue and improving mental
clarity. Also, dehydration can lead to nighttime
muscle cramps interrupting their sleep.

- _**Have a Snack**_ - A great way to ensure a restful night's sleep is by having a light snack before bed. Peanut butter toast with honey is an excellent choice as it combines carbohydrates and protein, which can help your body relax and drift off into deep slumber.

IN CONCLUSION, teen athletes must get enough restful sleep each night to maximize their physical and mental performance on the field or court. Good quality sleep helps improve overall physical performance by increasing energy levels, reducing fatigue, and improving reaction times, as well as aiding mental health by reducing stress and promoting positive thinking.

# CONCLUSION

In conclusion, this book clearly shows the importance of nutrition and its connection to mental health for teen athletes. Teen athletes must carefully consider their food selection and prioritize adequate sleep to perform at their best. The teenage athlete is an individual who must balance several essential elements of their health to reach optimal performance. Nutrition plays a vital role in this balance. You and your athlete need to tailor their nutritional needs for teenage athletes considering their age and gender and should consider physical activity level and food preferences. Evidence suggests that proper nutrition can positively affect mental health and athletic performance, making it essential for teenage athletes to assess their nutritional needs when making decisions about their lifestyle. Additionally, adequate sleep is critical for mental and physical well-being, so ensuring restful hours each night is essential for teen athletes. By creating a healthy lifestyle incorporating good nutrition and sufficient rest, teenage athletes can fuel their bodies with the energy they need to reach their goals.

I hope this book has helped illuminate the importance of nutrition in teenage athletes and how it contributes to mental health. By following the guidelines outlined here, teenage athletes can ensure they get all the essential nutrients necessary for optimal performance, both on and off the field. Healthy lifestyle choices are vital; proper nutrition, adequate rest, and physical activity are integral to a successful teen athlete's lifestyle. Ultimately, with a little extra effort and knowledge, teenage athletes can take control of their dietary needs and use them to improve their athletic performance while maintaining good mental health.

It is important to note that understanding the nuances between professional/amateur sports and the educational setting is crucial for creating individualized nutrition plans to optimize performance and ensure optimal physical and mental health outcomes. Ultimately, these considerations will benefit a successful sporting career - from youth to adult athletes.

The third book in the series takes a closer look at the physical activity of teen athletes. It builds on the concepts explored in the first two books by delving into how mental health links to an athlete's physical activity. This book offers readers a comprehensive guide to understanding how exercise, weight training, and other forms of physical activity affect teenage athletes' mental and physical development. It also provides practical advice on choosing activities that best fit individual needs, goals, and strategies for creating healthy habits that will last a lifetime.

Ultimately, this book, focused on nutrition. encourages and empowers athletes to gain a competitive advantage by paying attention to and understanding the importance of proper nutrition and how to successfully fuel the body while staying safe and getting the most out of each workout. By considering this vital aspect of nutrition athletes can gain increased metal toughness and reach their maximum potential as they prepare for the future.

# RESOURCES

## APPS, MEAL PLANS, AND MORE

### FOOD SHOPPING

These all provide a free version to help you make smart choices at the market:

MY FITNESS PAL: Allows you to scan barcodes on packaged foods, and some restaurant meals and enter foods to ensure you're getting all the nutrients you need.

**FOODUCATE** Scan barcodes or input foods manually. You'll get the total calories and an overview of the nutritional quality of the calories.

**SHOPWELL** Available in the App Store. Easy breakdown of nutrition labels to enable you to make good food choices.

## FOOD DELIVERY SERVICES:

### BEST OVERALL:
### TRIFECTA
*Pros:* Kitchen is peanut & gluten-free, meals can stay in freezer for 3mo, money back guarantee.
*Cons:* Meals are all chef's choice.

### BEST VALUE:
### FRESH N LEAN
*Pros:* Accommodates for allergies, a la Carte menu for all meals & snacks, free shipping.
*Cons:* Cannot mix & match meal plans, meals are all one serving.

### BEST HEAT & EAT:
### PETE'S REAL FOOD
*Pros:* Lots of veggies and high- quality protein, facilities are soy & gluten free.
*Cons:* No substitutions other than pork, more expensive than other meal plans.

### BEST FOR HIGH PROTEIN:
### FACTOR
*Pros:* Meals arrive fresh & fully prepared, most of the menu is low carb/keto friendly, ready in 2 minutes.
*Cons:* Meals are not customizable.

### BEST FOR PLANT-BASED:
### VEESTRO
*Pros:* Meals hold up in the freezer, high plant-based protein plan, Kosher plan available.
*Cons:* Flavor may be bland.

## BEST MEAL PREP PLANS:

These plans, unlike the meal delivery plans, you must cook yourself. Can we say, teaching your kiddo to cook the easy way?! Yes, yes we can!

### HOME CHEF:
*Pros:* Lots of options, easy to use packaging.
*Cons:* Salt, pepper, and oil not included.

### HELLO FRESH*
*Pros:* Easy to customize meals and skip weeks, easy-to-follow recipes. Accurate time for cooking/prep.
*Cons:* Cooking staples not included *Our son uses this one. He sends me photos of the meals he's cooked! It's nice to see him get excited about healthy food!

### EVERYPLATE
*Pros:* Big portions, reasonable price.
*Cons:* No vegan or other dietary restriction options.

### MARTHA STEWART & MARLEY SPOON
*Pros:* Delicious meals, easy directions, options for specific diets.
*Cons:* May not be available in all locations.

## BEST SLEEP APPS:

We all may have trouble sleeping at one time or another. Keeping a schedule on sleep and wake periods can be helpful. All are available in the App Store.

1. SLEEP CYCLE: Free version and premium for $29.99/mo. Helps track sleep habits and wakes you at the optimal time.
2. SLEEP SCORE: Free version and premium for $9.99/mo. Tracks sleep quality- No wearables needed!
3. HEADSPACE: Free version and premium for $12.99/mo. Soothing, guided meditation for relaxation and better sleep.
4. BREETHE*: $89.99/year. Help reduces stress, anxiety, and improve sleep.*My neighbor swears by this one!

## SUPPLEMENTS*:

### STRONG OG
*Vitamins, Minerals, & Vitamin D*

For years, our family has used "Strong OG", a liquid multivitamin clinically proven to reduce inflammation and improve immune function. Personally, I get very tired of taking pills! You take just 2oz per day. The shot glass is included in the box. When it's sweltering outside, I put 2oz in my water to help rehydrate. Furthermore, if anyone's coming down with something, we take more than 2oz per day. The product to buy is called STRONG OG under the "Strong & Ionic" tab on the website. Your best bet is to go onto an autoship, so you never run out. Additionally, we also enjoy the "Verve" product.

## BellaGrace Collagen

We take and love the collagen supplement from BellaGrace for our health. Clinically proven to improve joint mobility, increase endurance, and decrease recovery times, just to name a few benefits! A good idea is to go onto an autoship, so you never run out.

*\*Disclosure: I only recommend products I would use myself and with my family and all opinions expressed here are our own and are not to be confused with medical advice from a qualified physician. By purchasing these products, at no additional cost to you, I may earn a small commission.*

# YOUR BOOK REVIEW CAN MAKE A DIFFERENCE!

*Reviews are vital for independent authors. If you enjoyed this book, please take a moment to leave a quick review on Amazon—it makes a big difference! Even a short sentence helps. I appreciate your support and for being a part of this journey to elevate athletic performance and personal development. Together, we can make a difference in the lives of many athletes.*

Use this LINK/QR code to leave your ☆☆☆☆☆ review.

*Thank you!*

*LD Harris*

# BONUS MATERIAL

Athletes, take your performance to the next level by visiting our website! Discover a wealth of exclusive content tailored just for you, including expert tips, downloadable training documents, and more. Whether you're looking to enhance your skills, optimize your workouts, or stay motivated, our site offers valuable resources to help you achieve your goals. Don't miss out on this opportunity to elevate your game—explore now and unlock the benefits waiting for you!Tough Teen Athletes or follow us on Facebook and Instagram

# ABOUT THE AUTHOR

LD Harris is a Professional Sports Performance Professional, Certified Nutrition Counselor, and Certified Mental Toughness Trainer who is passionate about helping young athletes reach their fullest potential. As the parent of an elite high school athlete, 5x State Champion and 8x All-American, who became a Division I scholarship athlete, she understands the commitment that top-level success requires.

LD Harris' passion for nutrition, exercise, and mental grit has made her an indispensable asset to the lives of many athletes. With her experience as a Personal Trainer and Sports Performance and Nutrition consultant for the San Diego State

University Women's Swim Team, she has worked with countless individuals, athletes, and high school club teams to help athletes stay in peak form and outshine the competition. LD believes the same dedication and expertise can be used to achieve excellence outside of sports.

She serves as a trusted mentor and guide, helping individuals make informed decisions that will help them maximize their performance and reach their highest potential. Her sports performance consulting paired with her exercise science and nutrition expertise has earned LD a well-deserved reputation as one of the go-to sports performance specialists for anyone looking to improve their mental game, gain a competitive edge, and achieve their athletic goals.

## ALSO IN THIS SERIES

Mental Training for Teen Athletes

Mental Training for Teen Athletes- Nutrition

Mental Toughness for Teen Athletes-Food Log

Mental Toughness for Teen Athletes-Physical Training

Mental Toughness for Teen Athletes-Mental Training

Positive Affirmations for Male Teen Athletes

Positive Affirmations for Female Athletes

Young Athletes Mental Edge Code

You can find all our books on our website: Tough Teen Athletes-
Simply Scan this QR code:

Not in this Series:

11 High School Hacks* 11 Tips Teachers Wish Parents Knew About
Supporting Their Student

# REFERENCES

CDC. (2022, September 13). *Tips for better sleep.* Centers for Disease Control andPrevention.https://www.cdc.gov/sleep/about sleep/ sleep hygiene.html

Day Writing Journals. (2019 ). *Get enough sleep: Daily success, motivation and everyday inspiration for your best year ever, 365 days to more happiness motivational year long journal / daily notebook / diary.* Independently Published. https://health.gov/myhealthfinder/healthy-living/mental-health-and-rela tionships/get-enough-sleep

Grandner, M. A., Hall, C., Jaszewski, A., Alfonso-Miller, P., Gehrels, J.-A., Killgore, W. D. S., & Amy Athey. (2021). Mental Health in Student Athletes: Associations With Sleep Duration, Sleep Quality, Insomnia, Fatigue, and Sleep Apnea Symptoms. *Athletic Training & Sports Health Care, 13*(4), e15 9– e167. https://doi.org/10.3 9 28/19425864-20200521-01

*Sleep deprivation.* (n.d.). Cleveland Clinic. Retrieved June 22, 2023, from https:// my.clevelandclinic.org/health/diseases/239 70-sleep-deprivation

Why is sleep so important? (2014). *DukeMedicine Healthnews, 20*(8) , 8. https:// www.ncbi.nlm.nih.gov/pubmed/25233541

*Advice for parents of healthy-weight children.* (n.d.). Nhs.uk. Retrieved June 5, 2023, from https://www.nhs.uk/live-well/healthy-weight/childrens-weight/ healthy-weight-children-advice-for-parents

Ajmera, R., MS, & RD. (2018, October 17 ). *The vegetarian diet: A beginner's guide and meal plan.* Healthline. https://www.healthline.com/nutrition/vegetar ian-diet-plan

Braddock, J. (2021, May 25). *Protein Powder and Teenage Athletes ».* Off-Season Athlete.https://offseasonathlete.com/protein-powder-and-teenage- athletes

Brown, J. (2020, July 15). Is it safe to microwave food? *BBC.* https://www.bbc. com/future/article/20200714-is-it-safe-to-microwave-food

Brown, M. J., & (uk) , R. D. (2021, September 7 ). *What is organic food, and is it more nutritious than non-organic food?* Healthline. https://www.healthline. com/nutrition/what-is-organic-food

Bushell, J. (2022, April 20). *Eating Disorders a Danger for Competitive Young Athletes.* MEDA - Multi-Service Eating Disorders Association. https://www. medainc.org/eating-disorders-a-danger-for-competitive-young-athletes

Campbell, E. (2019 , November 7 ). *Carbohydrates to fuel young athletes.* Youth Sport Nutrition. https://youthsportnutrition.com/blogs/teamysn-forum/ carbohydrates-to-fuel-young-athletes

Cassandra Calabrese, D. O. (2022, December 30). *11 Foods That Boost Your Immune System*. Cleveland Clinic. https://health.clevelandclinic.org/food-to-boost-your-immune-system

Children's Health. (n.d.-a). *Importance of Hydration for Young Athletes - Children's Health*. Retrieved June 4, 2023, from https://www.childrens.com/ health-wellness/the-importance-of-hydration-for-young-athletes

Children's Health. (n.d.-b). *Prevent dehydration in young athletes - children's health*. Retrieved June 4, 2023, from https://www.childrens.com/health- wellness/dehydration-can-sneak-up-on-athletes

CHOC. (2019a, February 5). *Protein powders and teens: Are they safe? Are they necessary?* CHOC - Children's Health Hub; CHOC. https://health.choc.org/ protein-powders-and-teens-are-they-safe

CHOC. (2019b, October 3). *How to help your child develop a healthy relationship with food*. CHOC - Children's Health Hub; CHOC. https://health.choc.org/ how-to-help-your-child-develop-a-healthy-relationship-with-food

*Classification of physical activity and level of intensity*. (n.d.). Retrieved June 4, 2023, from https://www.change4health.gov.hk/en/physical_activity/facts/ classification/index.html

*Developing positive attitudes toward food*. (n.d.). Retrieved June 6, 2023, from https://www.education.ne.gov/ns/cacfp/foodnutrition/developing-posi tive-attitudes-toward-food

*Dietary supplements & young athletes: Unravelling fact from fiction*. (n.d.). Retrieved June 8, 2023, from https://www.nationwidechildrens.org/special ties/sports-medicine/sports-medicine-articles/dietary-supplements-and- young-athletes

*Eating disorders: About more than food*. (n.d.). National Institute of Mental Health (NIMH). Retrieved June 6, 2023, from https://www.nimh.nih.gov/ health/publications/eating-disorders

*Eating to boost energy*. (2011, July 26). Harvard Health. https://www.health. harvard.edu/healthbeat/eating-to-boost-energy

*Effects of dehydration on athletic performance*. (2020, July 24). Spooner Physical Therapy; Spooner. https://www.spoonerpt.com/spooner-blog/effects-dehy dration-athletic-performance

*Follow the athlete diet*. (n.d.). Sunwarrior. Retrieved June 3, 2023, from https:// sunwarrior.com/blogs/health-hub/most-important-foods-athletes-should- avoid

*Grass-fed beef: Is it good for you?* (n.d.). WebMD. Retrieved June 3, 2023, from https://www.webmd.com/diet/grass-fed-beef-good-for-you

*GreenSmoothieGirl - achieve extraordinary health!* (2018, September 20). Green-SmoothieGirl; Robyn Openshaw. https://greensmoothiegirl.com/

Griebeler, M. (2021, October 5). *Is It Bad to Lose Weight Too Fast?* Cleveland Clinic. https://health.clevelandclinic.org/risks-of-losing-weight-too-fast

Helen West, R. D. (2022, July 26). *Electrolytes: Definition, functions, imbalance and sources*. https://www.healthline.com/nutrition/electrolytes

Infront, G. (2019, May 6). *Dietary Fat*. U.S. Anti-Doping Agency (USADA). https://www.usada.org/athletes/substances/nutrition/fat

J ulson, E., MS, RDN, & CLT. (2019, January 8). *Celiac disease diet: Food lists, sample menu, and tips*. Healthline. https://www.healthline.com/nutrition/celiac-disease-diet

Kadey, M. (2022, March 10). *The 6 best energy-dense foods to fuel your workouts*. Runner's World. https://www.runnersworld.com/nutrition-weight-loss/a3938704.7/energy-density-foods/

Kay, I. (2019, October 21). *Is your mood disorder a symptom of unstable blood sugar?* University of Michigan School of Public Health. https://sph.umich.edu/pursuit/2019posts/mood-blood-sugar-kujawski.html

Lumen Learning. (n.d.). *Cognitive development during adolescence*. Retrieved June 2, 2023, from https://courses.lumenlearning. com/wm-lifespandevelopment/chapter/cognitive-development-during-adolescence

*Mental toughness: The key to athletic success*. (n.d.). Retrieved June 2, 2023, from https://www.trine.edu/academics/centers/center-for-sports-studies/blog/2021/mental toughness the key to athletic success.aspx

Muinos, L. (2011, April 1). *What is a raw food diet?* Verywell Fit. https://www.verywellfit.com/food-to-eat-on-the-raw-food-diet-89 9 21

*Nutrition for Teens*. (2022, November 4). https://www.sharp.com/health-news/common-myths-about-teen-nutrition

*Protein for the teen athlete*. (n.d.). HealthyChildren.org. Retrieved June 3, 2023, from https://www.healthychildren.org/English/ages-stages/teen/nutrition/Pages/Protein-for-the-Teen-Athlete.aspx

Purcell, L. K., & Canadian Paediatric Society, Paediatric Sports and Exercise Medicine Section. (2013). Sport nutrition for young athletes. *Paediatrics & Child Health, 18*(4), 200–205. https://doi.org/10.1093/pch/18.4.200

Rizzo, N. (2016, June 21). *The ultimate guide to feeding vegan athletes*. Greenletes. https://greenletes.com/vegan-athlete-diet

*Safe weight loss and weight gain for young athletes*. (n.d.). HealthyChildren.org. Retrieved June 6, 2023, from https://www.healthychildren.org/English/healthy-living/sports/Pages/Safe-Weight-Loss-and-Weight-Gain-for- Young-Athletes.aspx

Shereen Lehman, M. S. (2005, November 12). *Complete protein combinations for vegans*. Verywell Fit. https://www.verywellfit.com/vegan-protein-combinations-25063 9 6

*Statista - the statistics portal*. (n.d.). Statista. Retrieved June 15, 2023, from http://www.statista.com

Teen sports and mental health: 10 mental benefits of sports. (2021, December 8).

*Newport Academy*. https://www.newportacademy.com/resources/ mental-health/sports-and-mental-health

*The Low FODMAP Diet: A Benefit for Athletes?* (n.d.). Retrieved June 11, 2023, from https://coach.ca/low-fodmap-diet-benefit-athletes

Tinsley, G., CSCS, *D, & CISSN. (2018, May 13). *Sports drinks: Should you drink them instead of water?* Healthline. https://www.healthline.com/nutrition/sports-drinks[1]

*Vegan diet: Foods, benefits & more.* (n.d.). WebMD. Retrieved June 11, 2023, from https://www.webmd.com/diet/vegan-diet-overview

*Water vs. Sports drinks.* (n.d.). Retrieved June 8, 2023, from https://www.chil drenscolorado.org/conditions-and-advice/sports-articles/sports-nutrition/ water-vs-sports-drinks-which-is-better-for-young-athletes/

Website, N. H. S. (n.d.). *Advice for parents – Eating disorders.* Nhs.uk. Retrieved J une 6, 2023, from https://www.nhs.uk/mental-health/feelings-symptoms-behaviours/behaviours/eating-disorders/advice-for-parents

*Why stable blood sugar matters.* (2021, September 9). UCAN. https://ucan.co/stable-blood-sugar

UCAN; Generation Wynn, K. (2020, July 27). *The 5 best (and 3 worst) fats you can possibly eat during training.* Spartan Race. https://www.spartan.com/blogs/ unbreakable-train ing/fats-to-eat-during-training

Dehydration. (n.d.). Cleveland Clinic. Retrieved June 15, 2023, from https://my. clevelandclinic.org/health/treatments/9013-dehydration

Diabetes diet, eating, & physical activity. (2023, June 7). National Institute of Diabetes and Digestive and Kidney Diseases; NIDDK - National Institute of Diabetes and Digestive and Kidney Diseases. https://www.niddk.nih. gov/health-information/diabetes/overview/diet-eating-physical-activity

Kohl, H. W., III, Cook, H. D., Committee on Physical Activity and Physical Education, Food and Nutrition Board, & Institute of Medicine. (2013). Physical Activity and Physical Education: Relationship to Growth, Development, and Health. National Academies Press (US). https://www.ncbi. nlm.nih.gov/books/NBK201497/

Popkin, B. M., D'Anci, K. E., & Rosenberg, I. H. (2010). Water, hydration, and health. Nutrition Reviews, 68(8), 439–458. https://doi.org/10.1111/j.1753-4887. 2010.00304.x

Bringhurst, Robert. *The Elements of Typographic Style.* Version 3.2. Point Roberts: Hartley & Marks, 2004.

Very Well Fit: https://www.verywellfit.com/best-meal-delivery-services-for-fitness-5195409

NY Times Post: https://nypost.com/article/the-best-meal-delivery-kits/

*The Chicago Manual of Style.* 17th ed. The University of Chicago Press Editorial

Staff. Chicago: The University of Chicago Press, 2017. https://www.chicago manualofstyle.org/.

*Vellum Tutorial.* Updated regularly. Oakland and Seattle: 180g. https://help. vellum.pub/tutorial/.

Made in the USA
Las Vegas, NV
21 May 2025

22475353R00105